Cayman Islands

Picture Book

Cayman Islands

Picture Book

Andrea Hoff-Domin

1.   Edition 2015—English

Photographs by Florida Services & Information LLC

Map by Microsoft map point

Cover photograph by Florida Services & Information LLC, Fort Lauderdale, Florida

ISBN: 098625293X

ISBN-13: 978-09862529-3-8

National Motto of the Cayman Islands

He hath founded it upon the seas.

About the Author

Born on October 6 in lower Saxony, Germany, Andrea Hoff-Domin lost her father when she was a baby, and life with her new stepfather was never easy. Books about foreign countries and their culture were her escape from everyday life and inspired her enthusiasm for the wide world. Her grandparents, especially her grandfather, had a big influence on her. He was an architect, and she accompanied him on his trips to construction sites and sat at his feet when he was drawing houses. At that time, she developed her passion for houses and properties, which is her main profession today. She runs an international brokerage in Florida and is known as a Florida expert. To fulfill her lifelong dream, she started her career as a financial specialist in the biggest German bank and renovated condominiums. During that time, she began to write for several magazines and Internet portals. She lives by the motto "Do or do not; there is no try" (Yoda, Star Wars).

www.florida-dream-homes.net
www.andreahoffdomin.com
andrea@florida-informations.com

Cayman Islands

For business people and real estate investors we have our informative book about the business opportunities in the Cayman Islands. To give vacationers and tourists the chance to see this beautiful island, we put together a selection of our photographs. Enjoy!

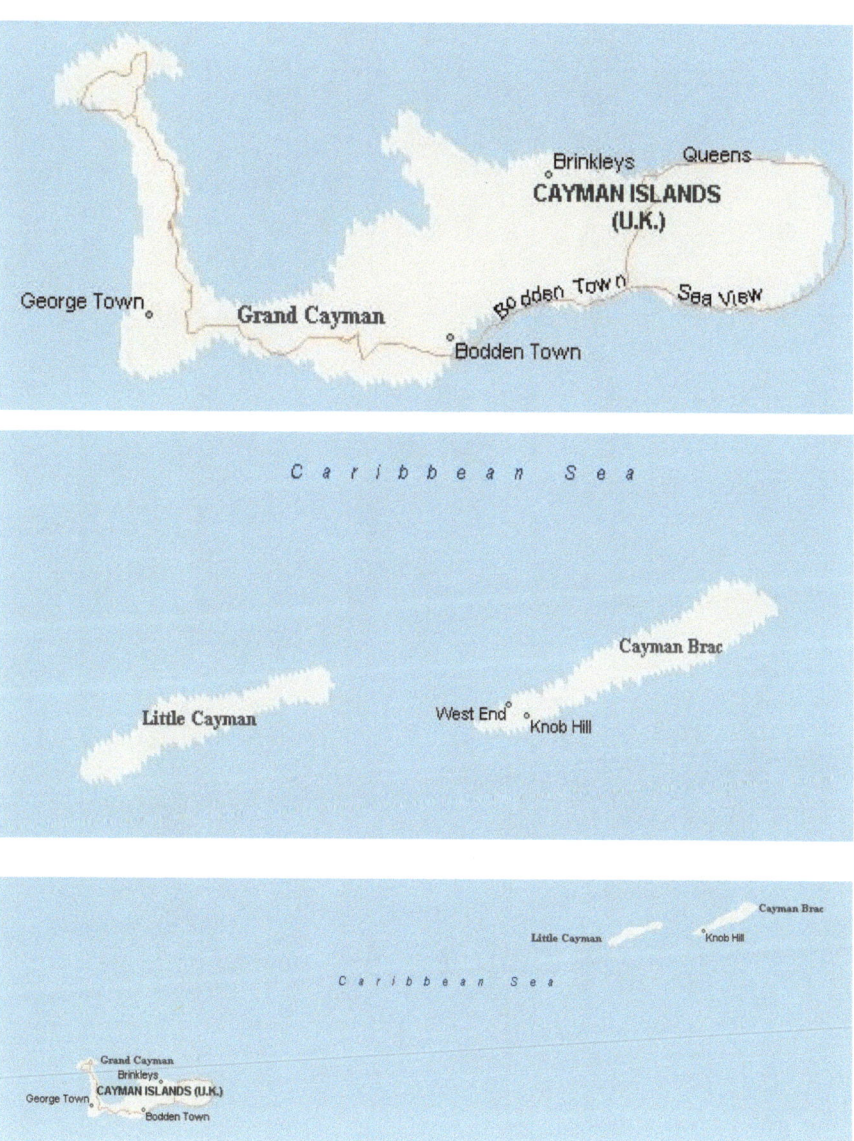

Natural Treasure Selection from the Cayman Islands

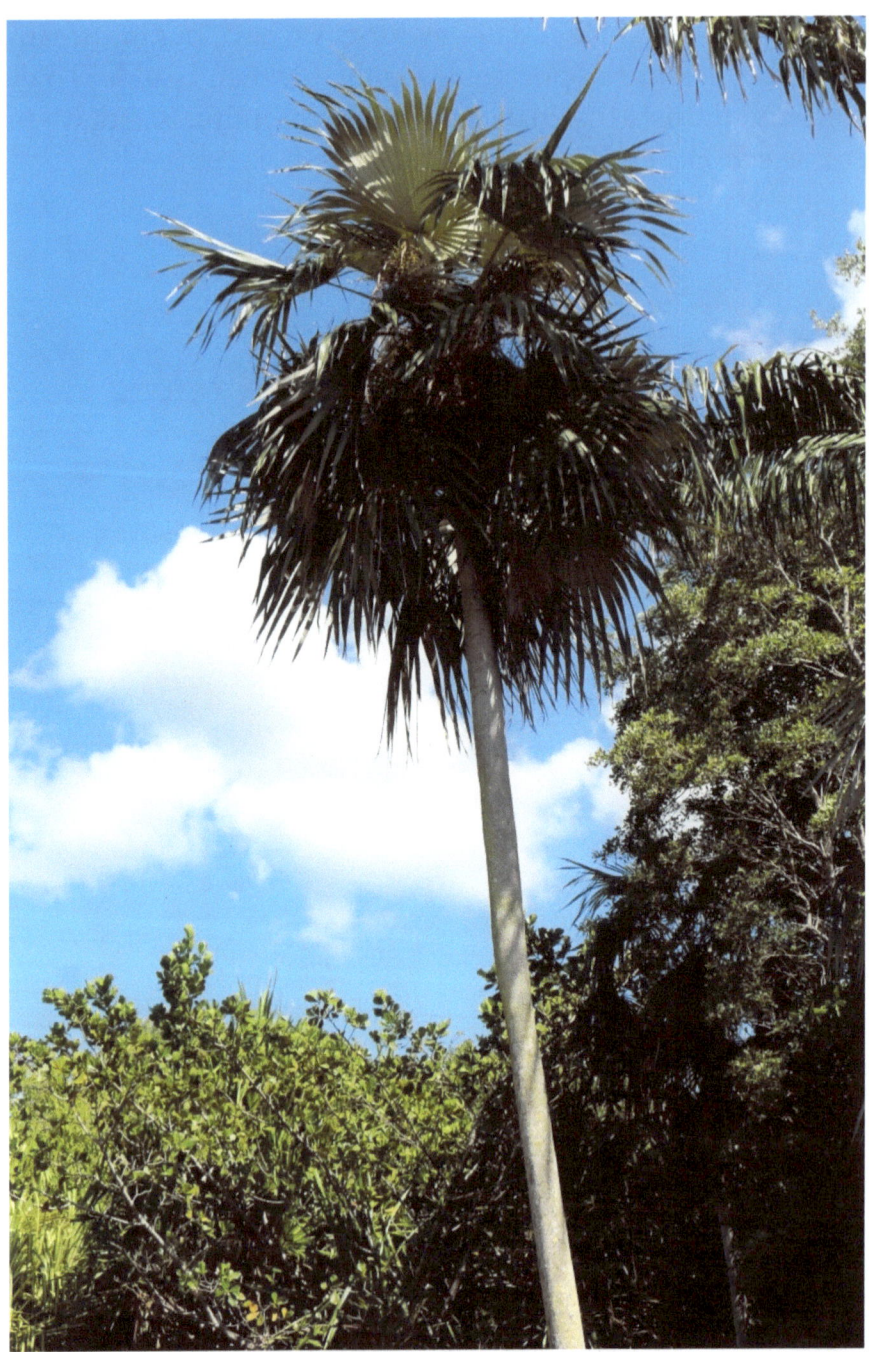

The Silver Thatch Palm tree – the national tree

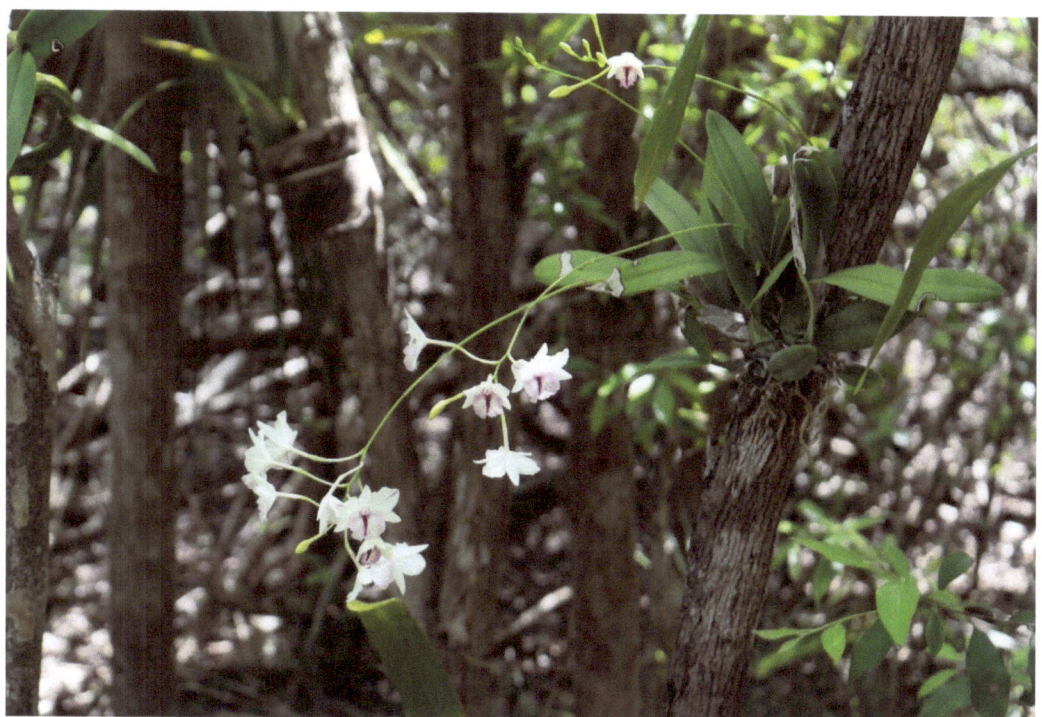

Orchids in the Botanic Garden

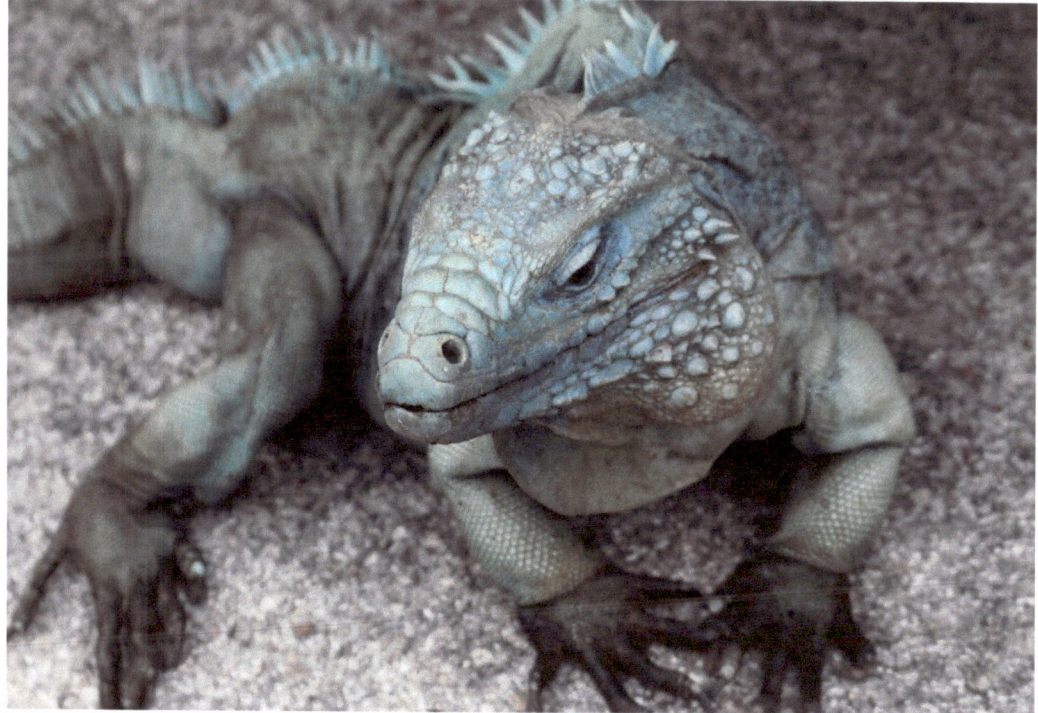

The Blue Iguana

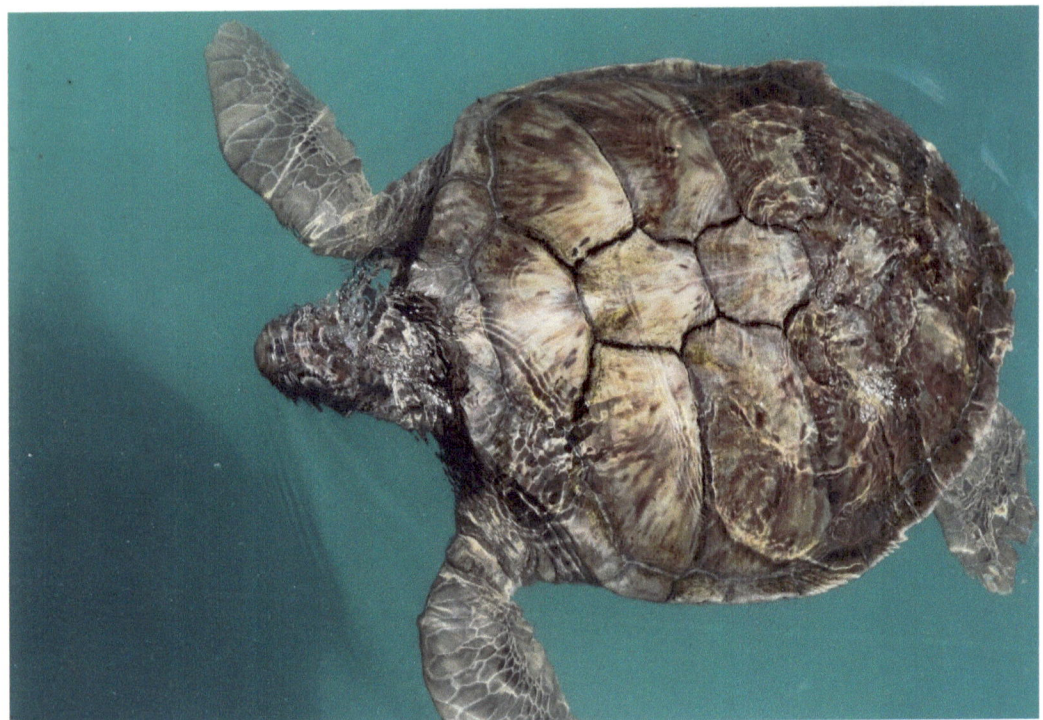

The Green Sea Turtle – National Animal

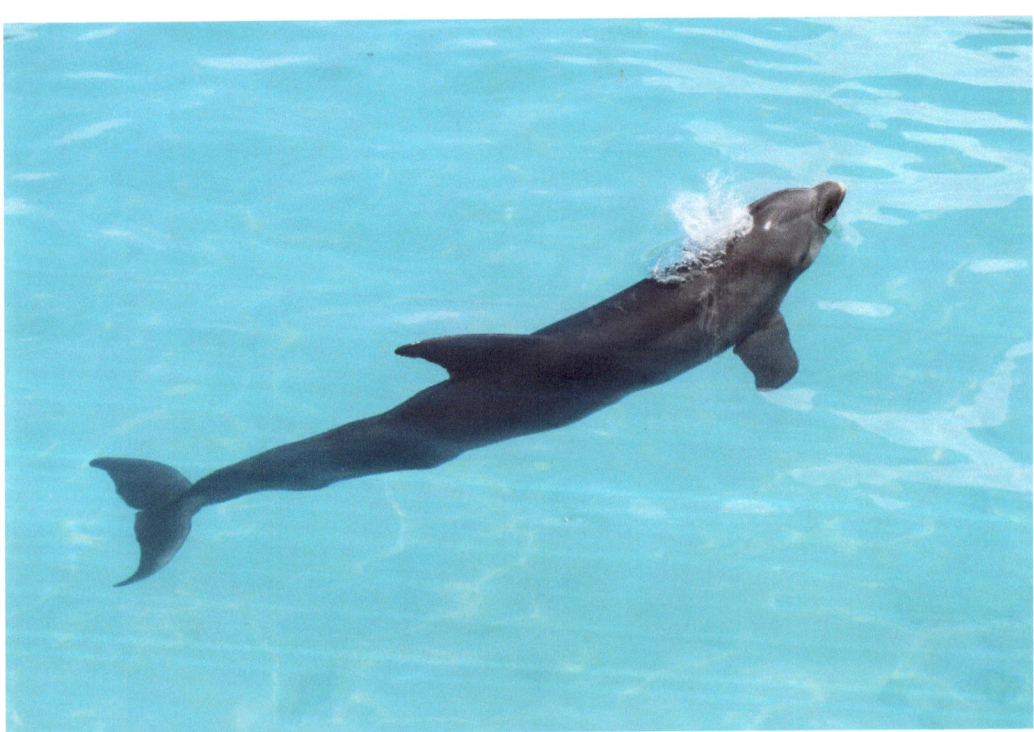

Dolphin in Dolphin Cove

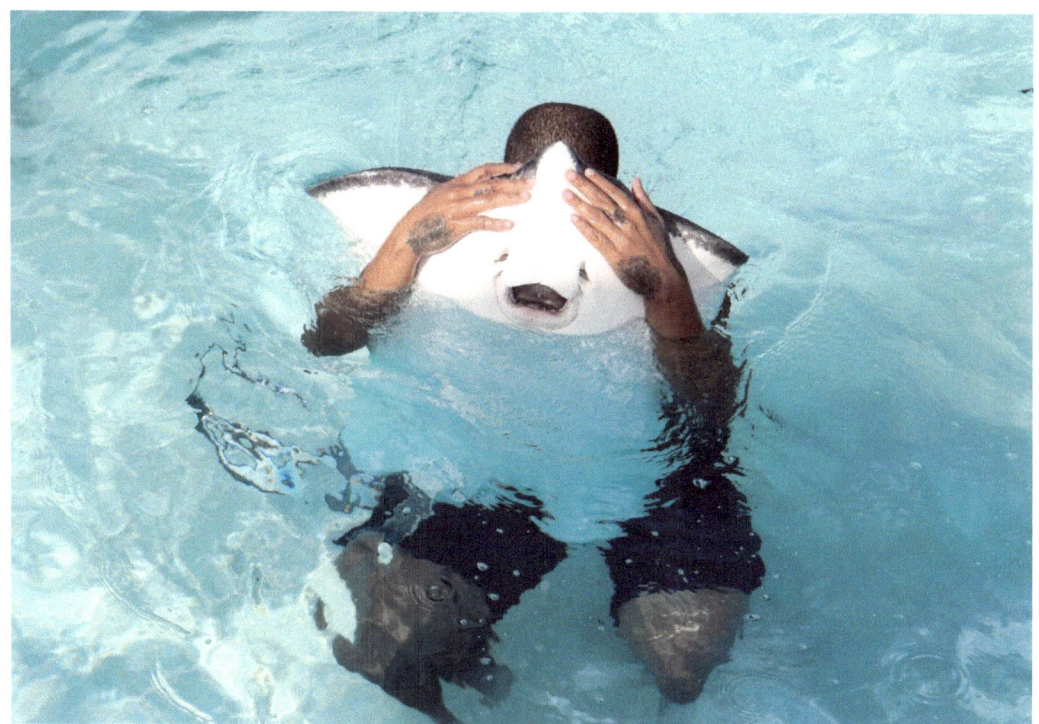

Play with a Stingray

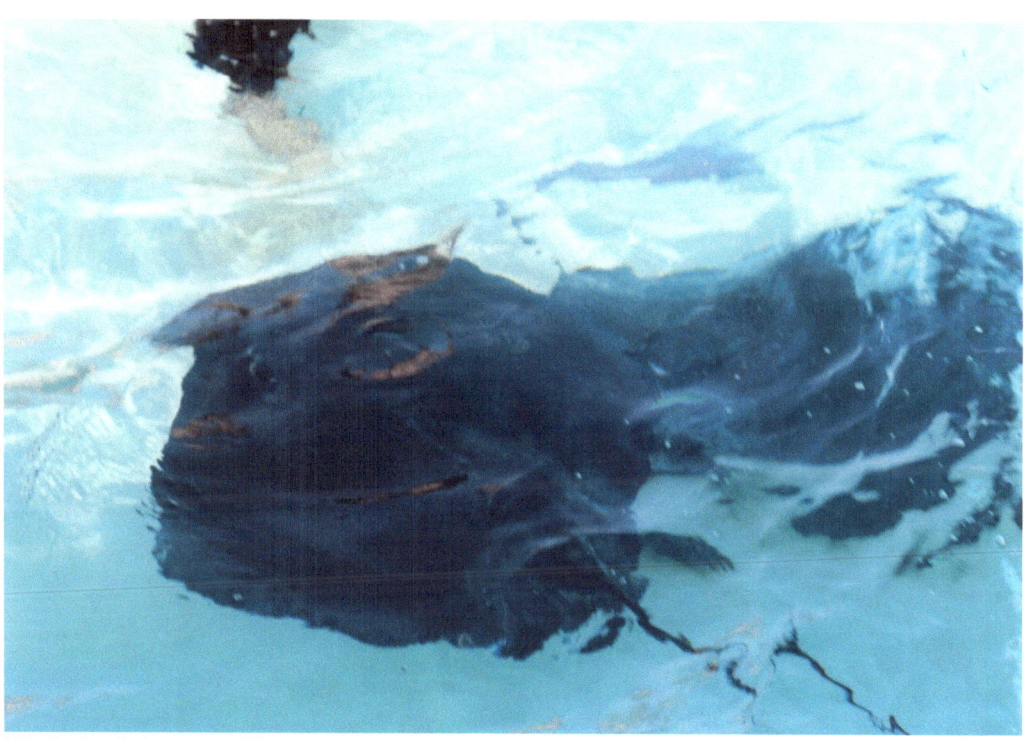

Visit in Stingray City

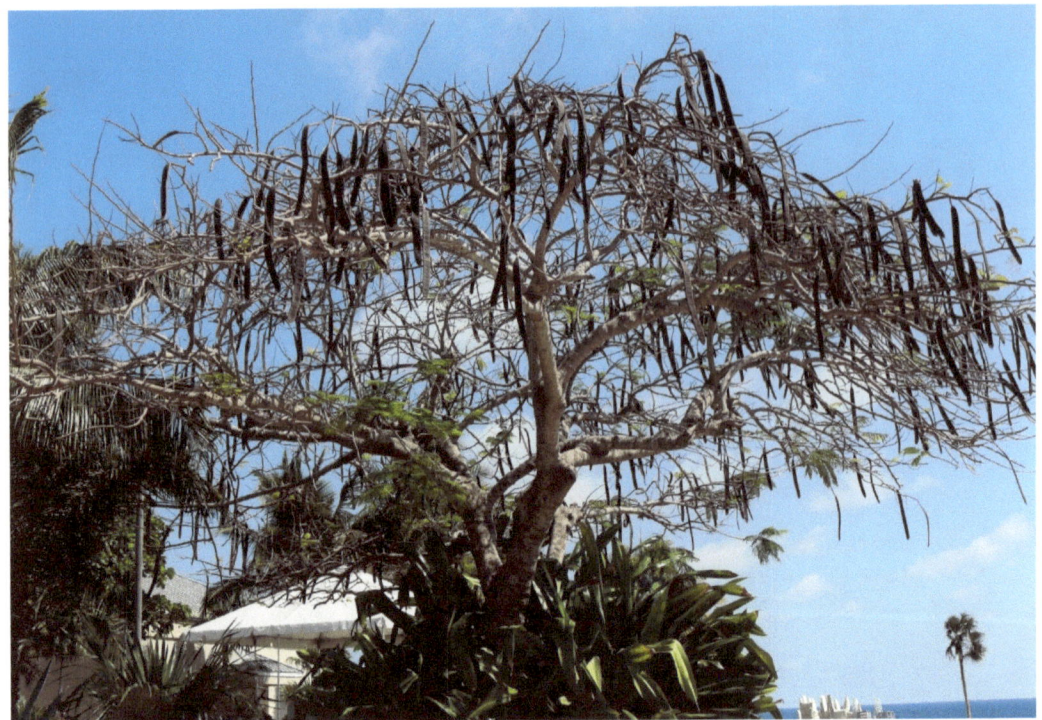

Tamarind Tree – ready to harvest the Fruits

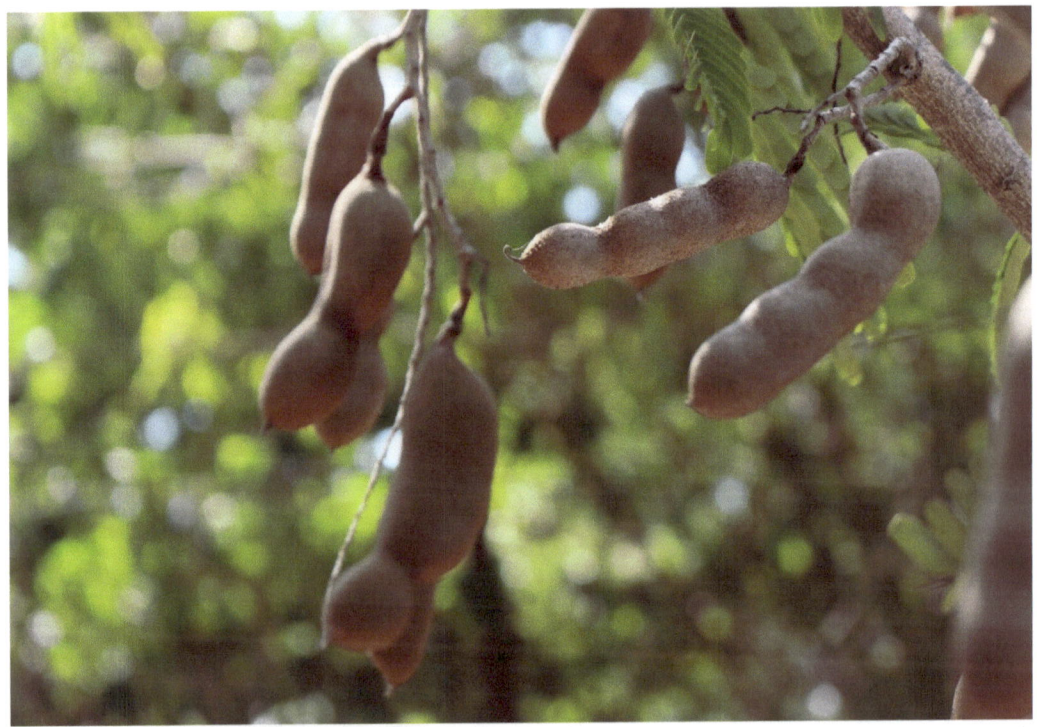

Tamarind Fruits – sour-sweet, sticky Delicacy

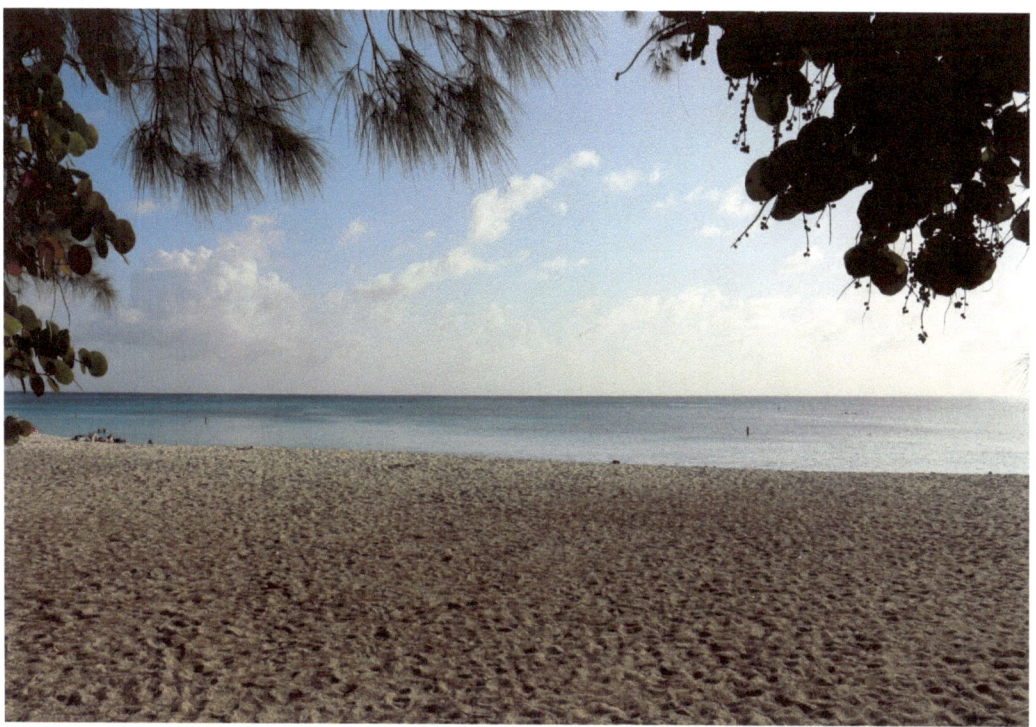

Secluded Beach

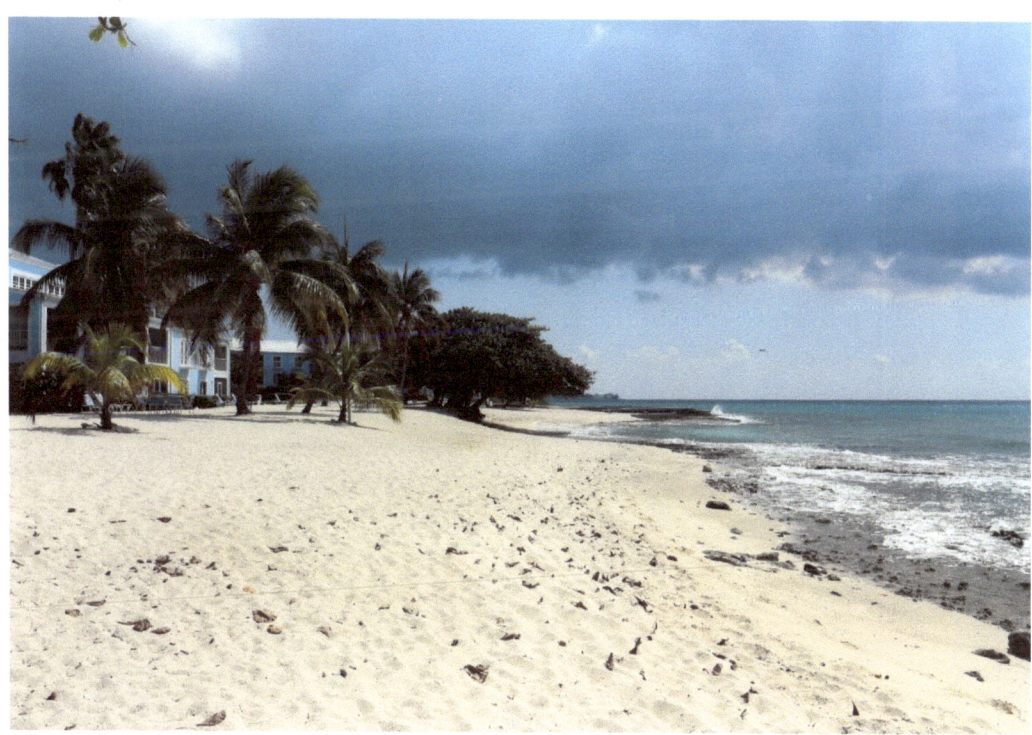

Your Beach in front of you Beach Condominium

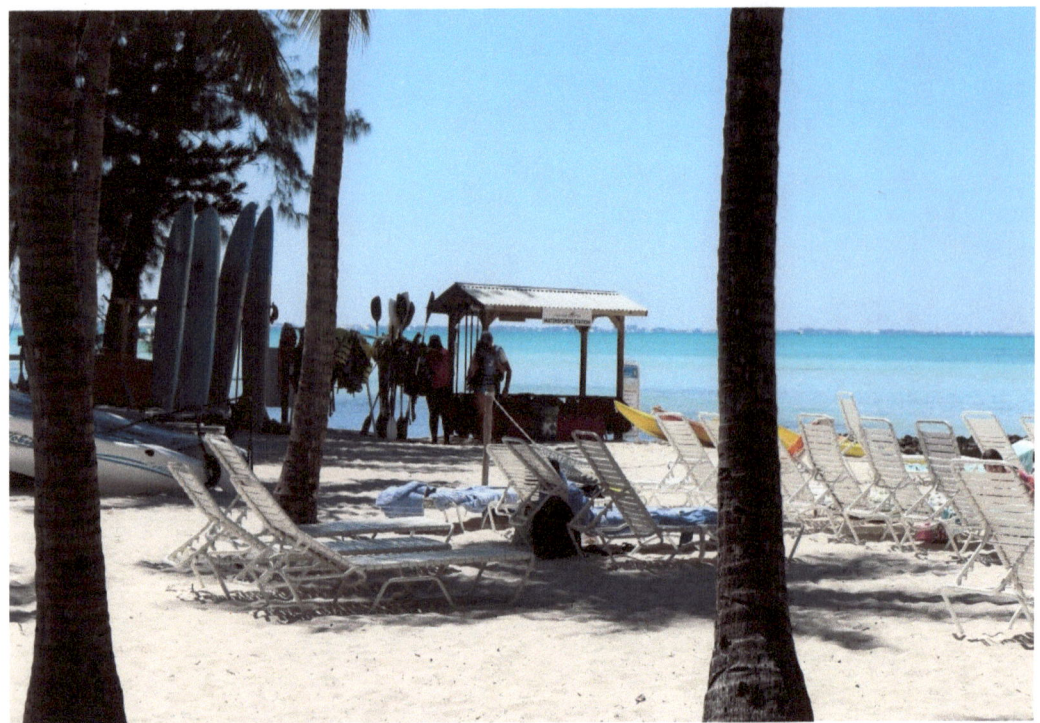

Rum Point invites you for a Day in the Sun

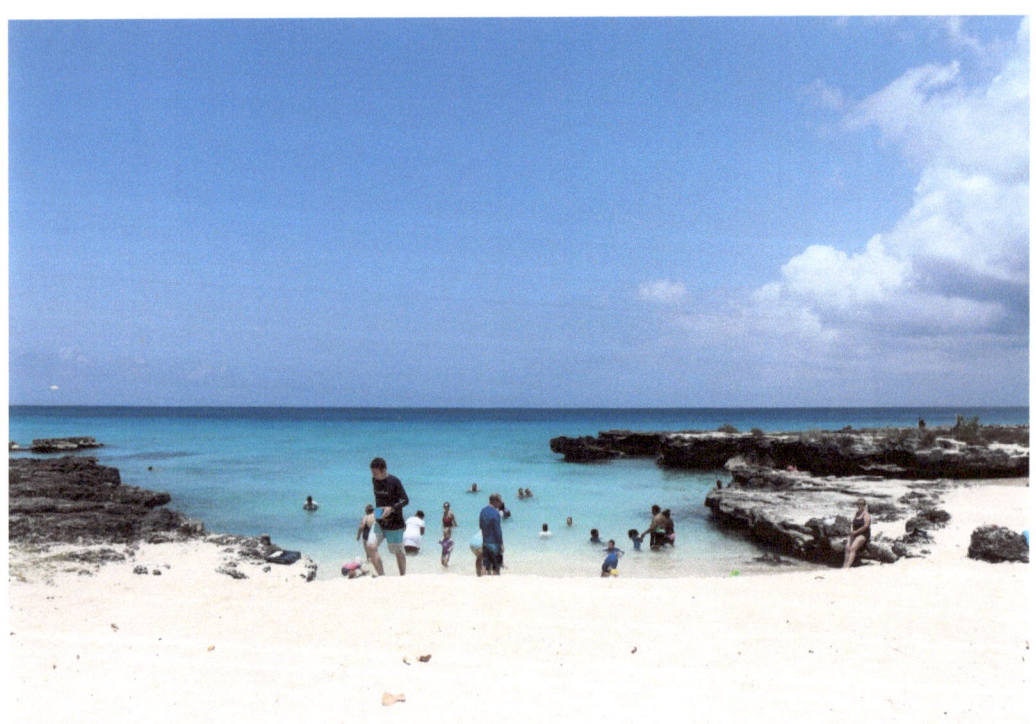

Sunday's Family Fun at the Beach

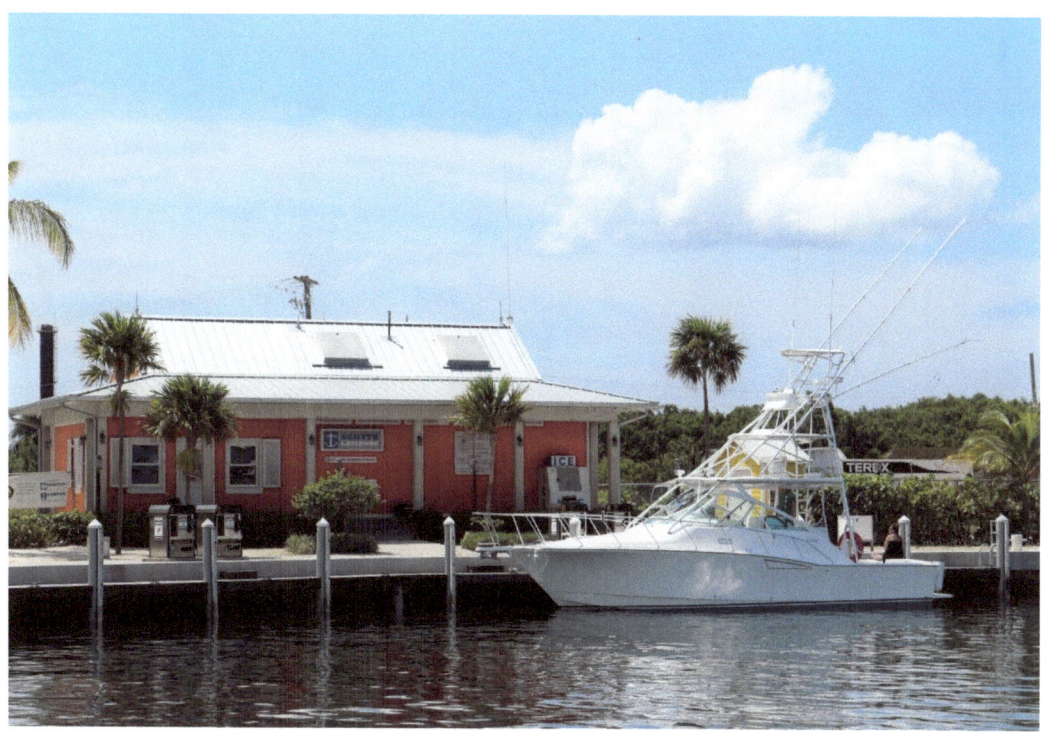

Marina Scene

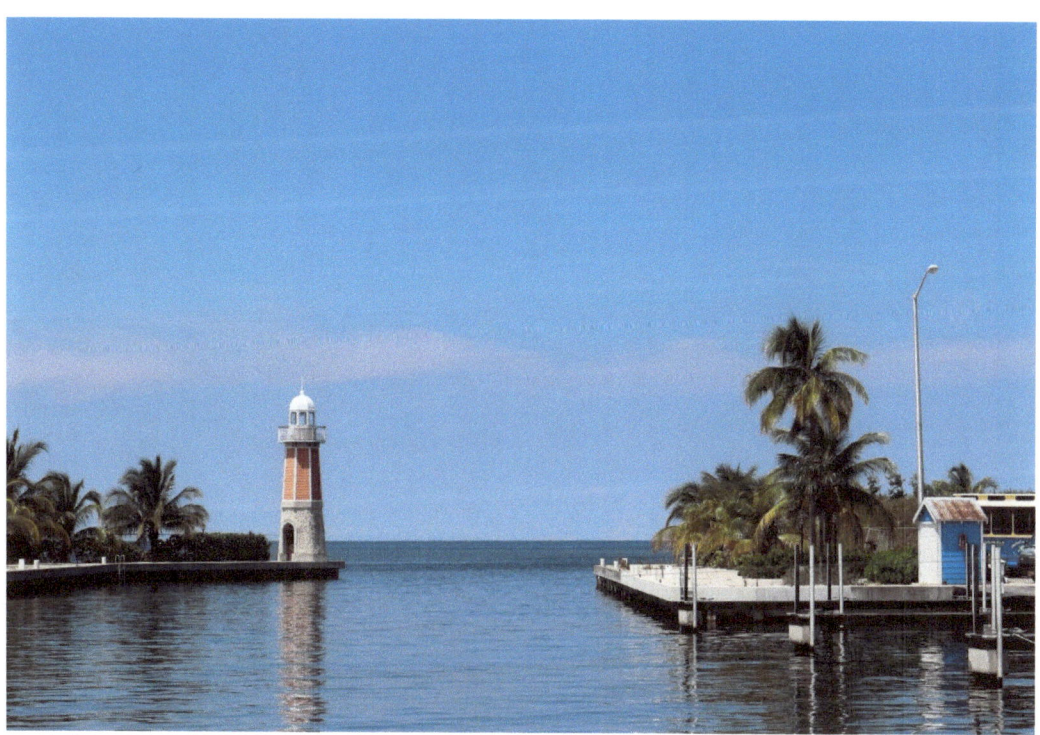

On your Way into the Lagoon

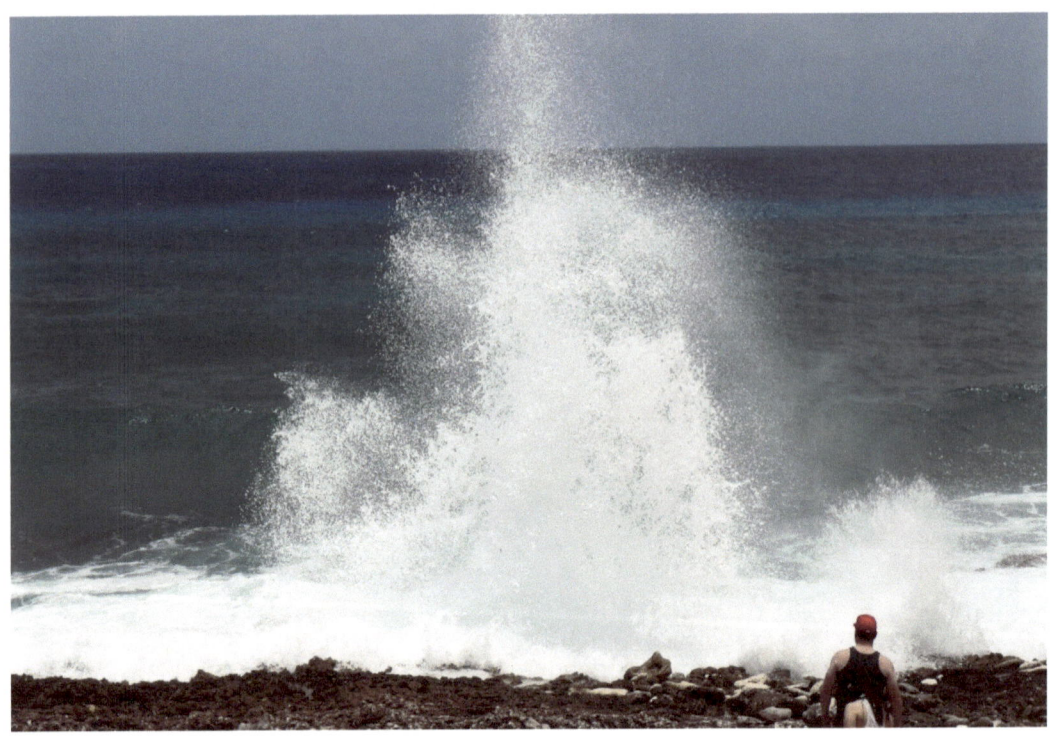

Blow Holes and Nature Beach at the South Coast

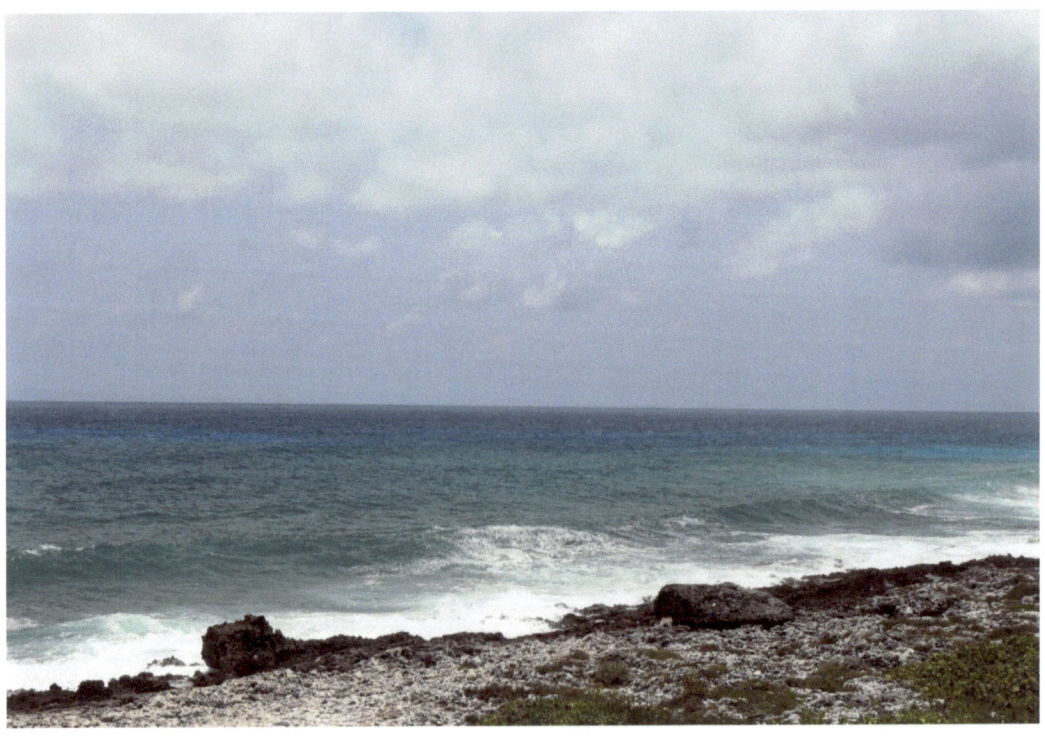

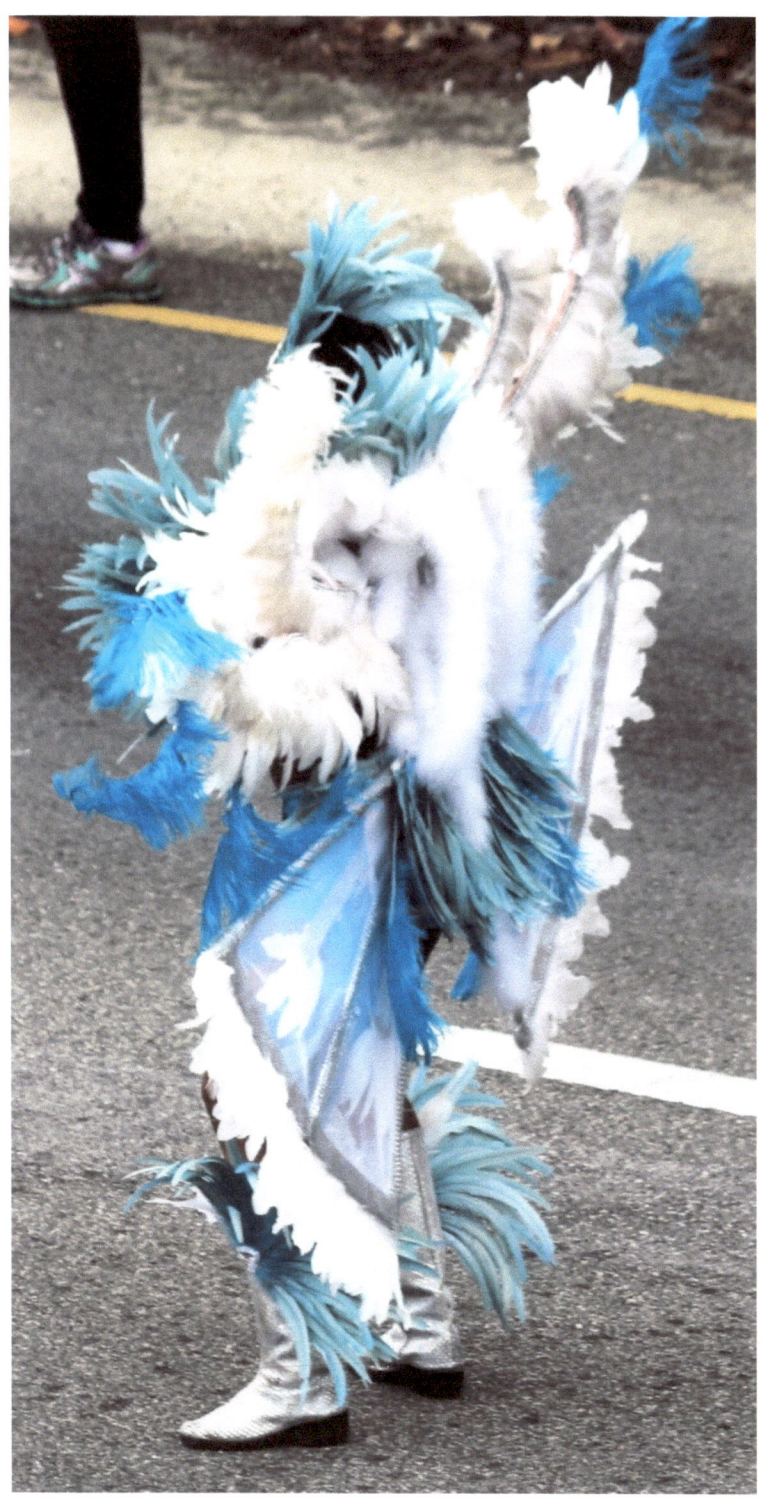

Batabano Parade

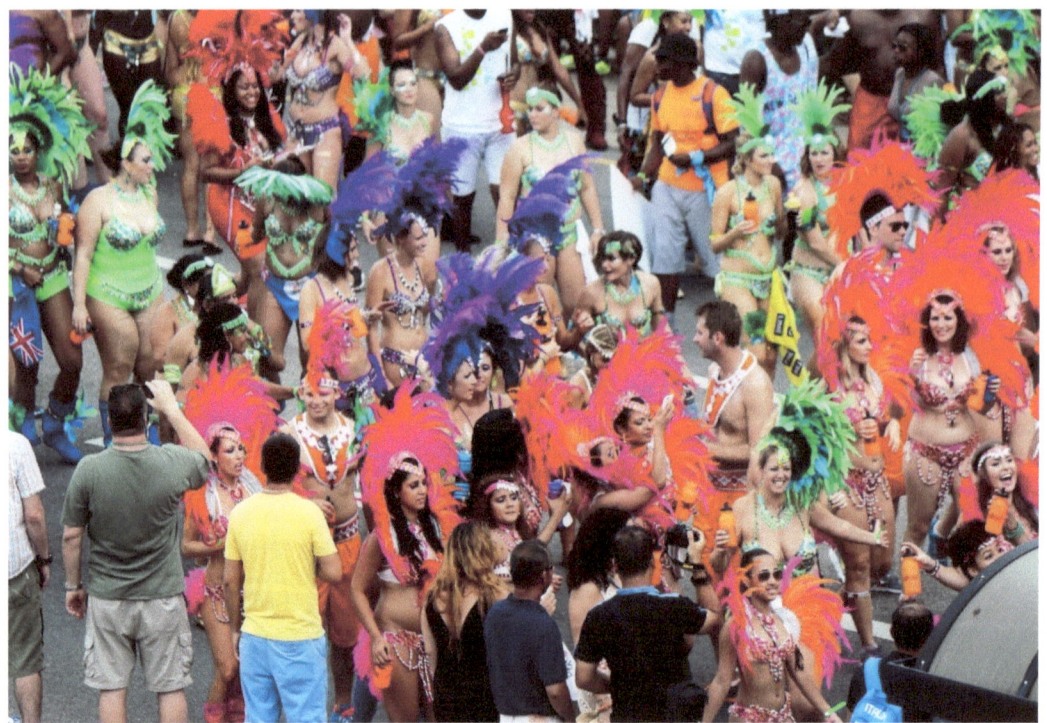

Batabano Parade

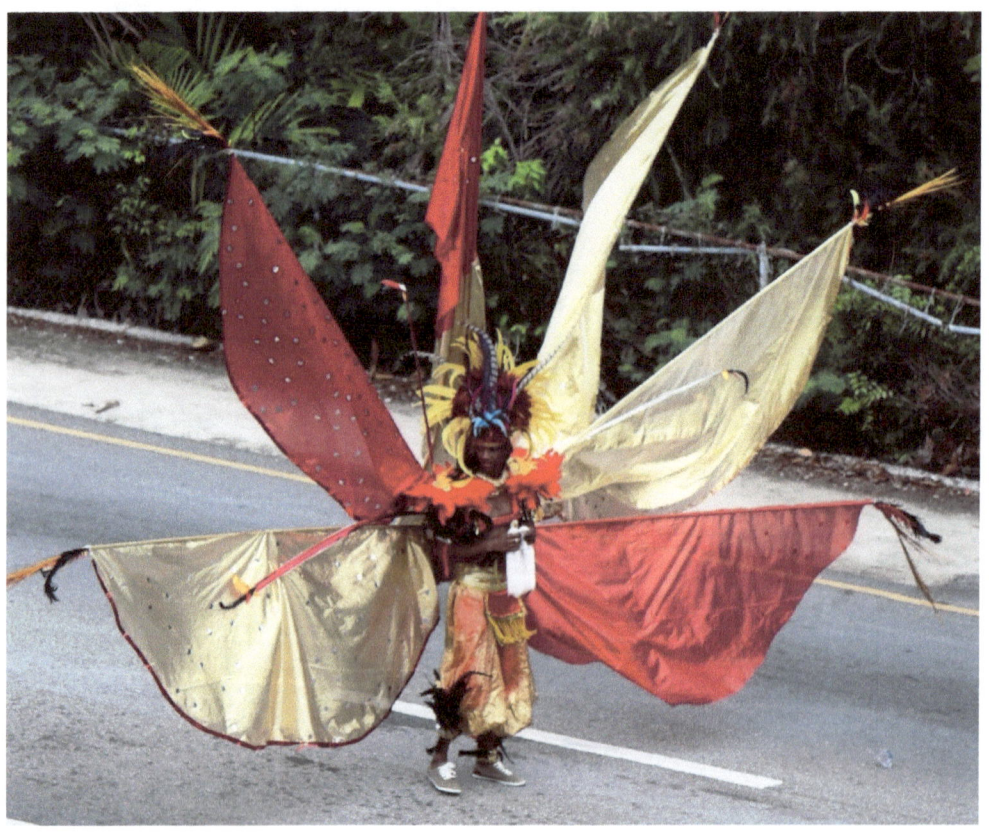

Attractions in Grand Cayman

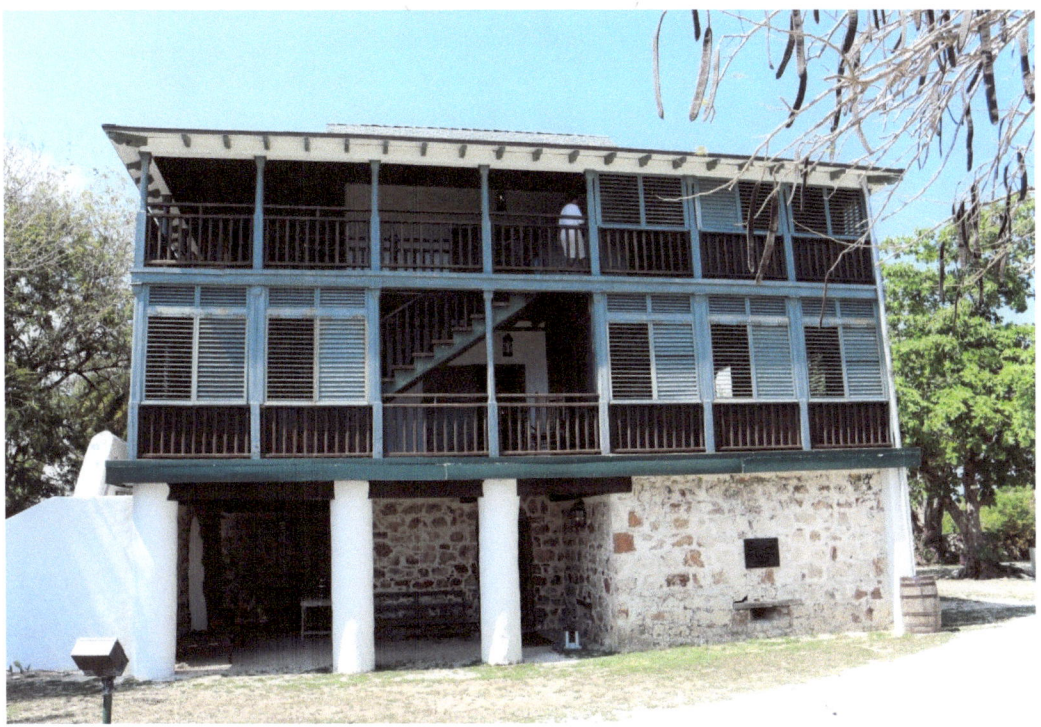

The oldest Building – Pedro St. James Castle

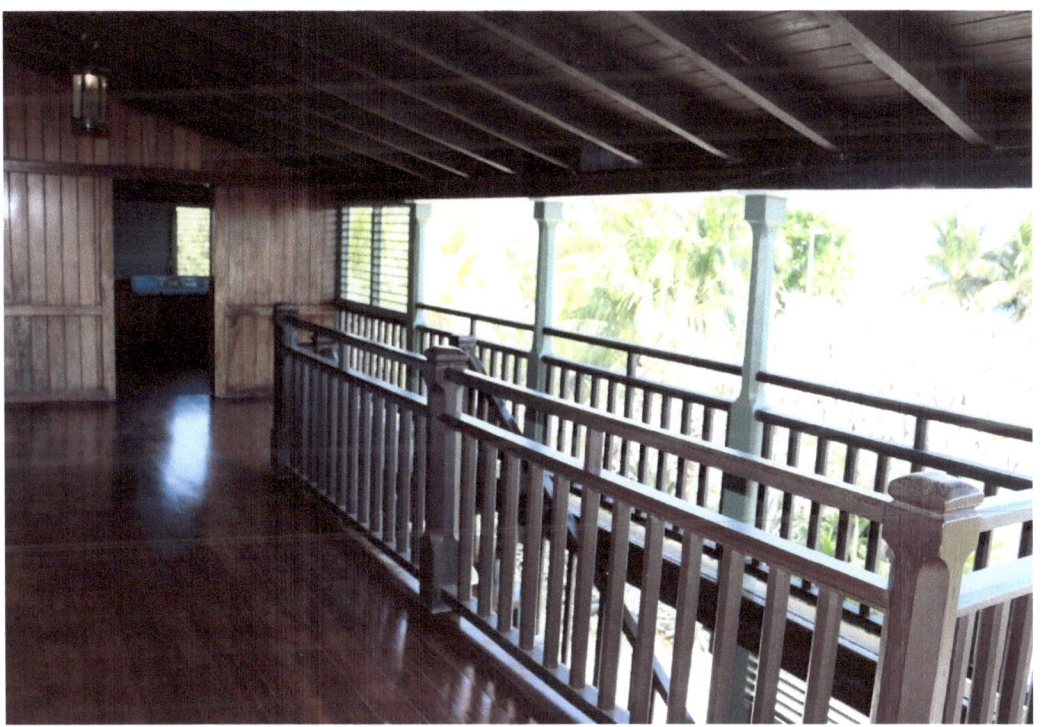

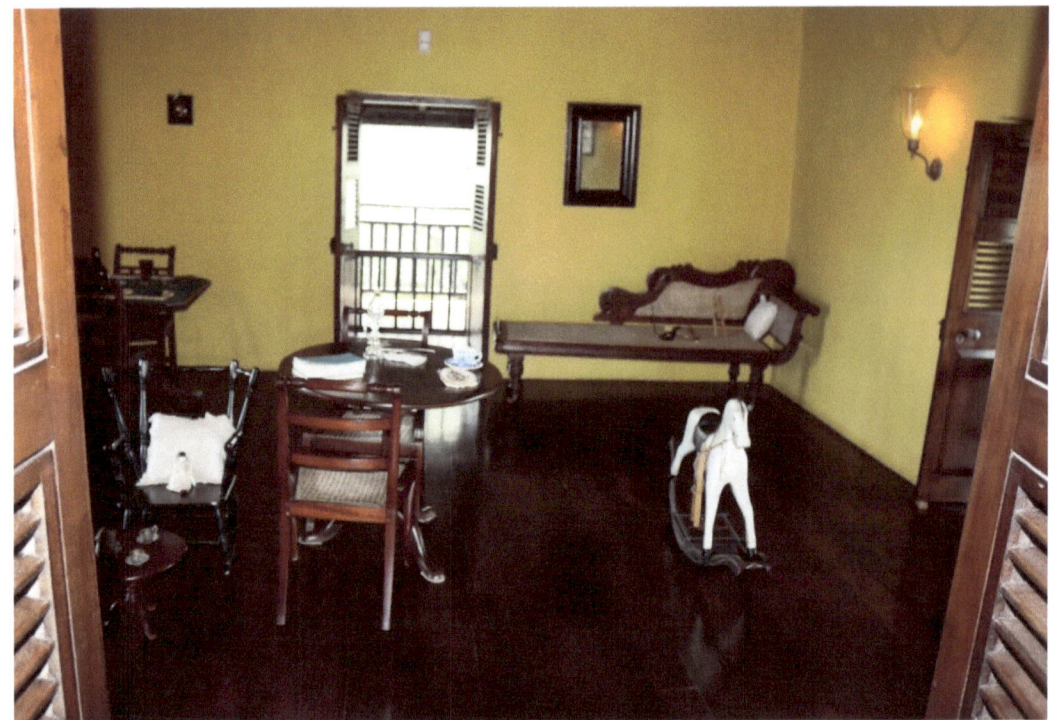

Living Area 3rd Floor – Pedro St. James

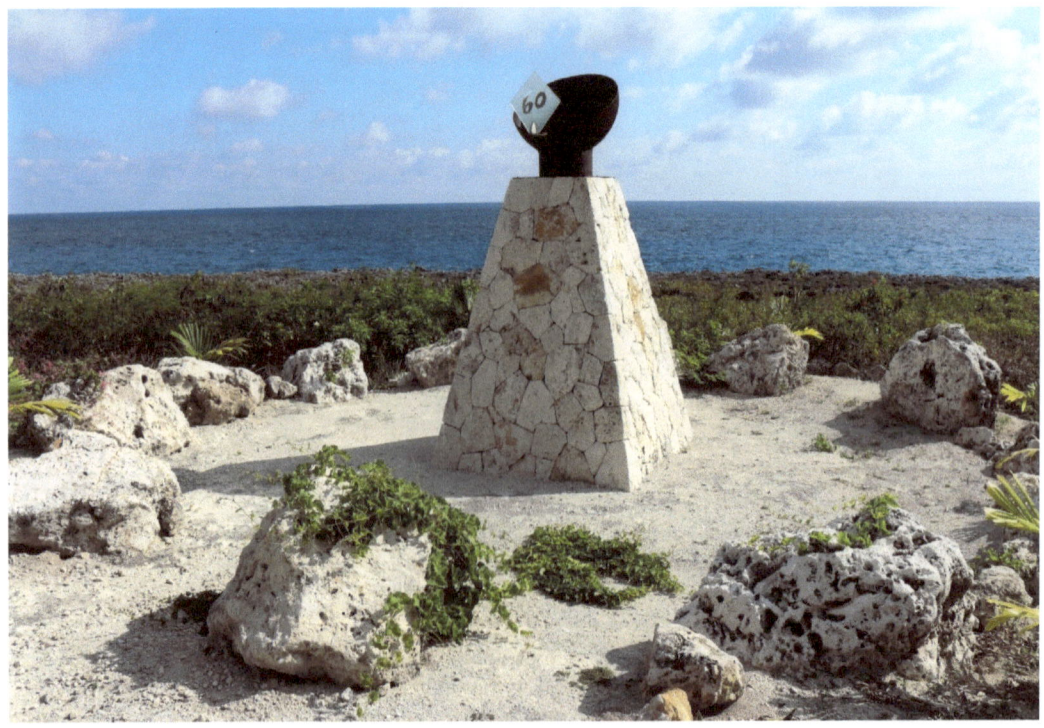

Garden with Monument – Pedro St. James

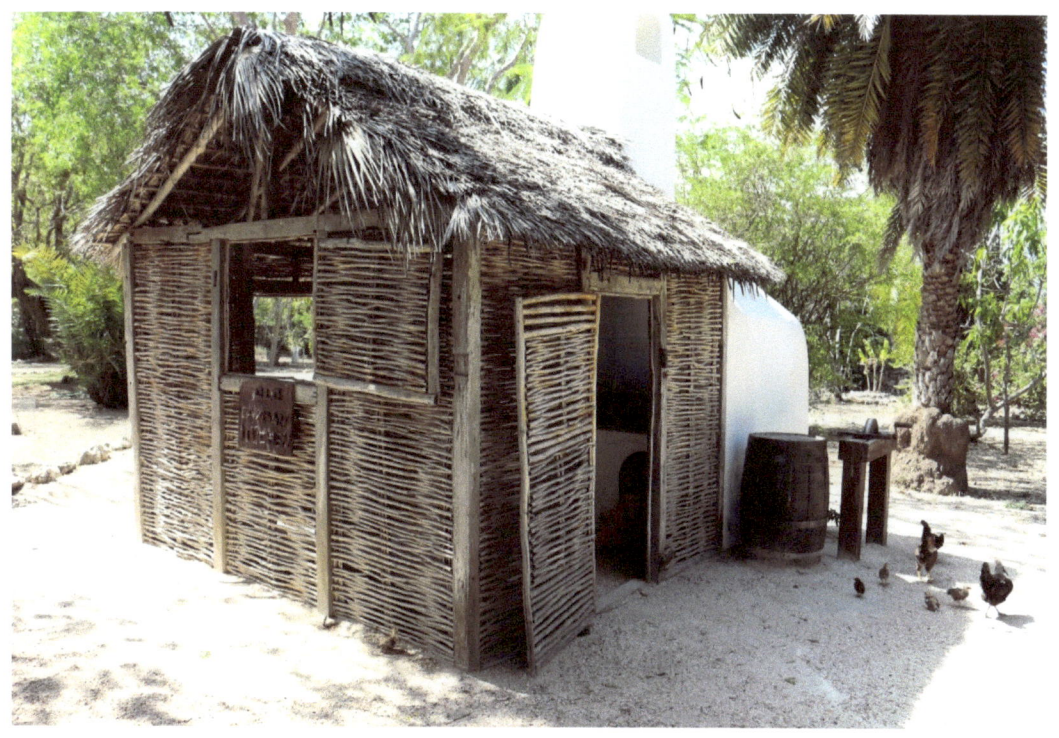

Kaboose (Kitchen) – Pedro St. James

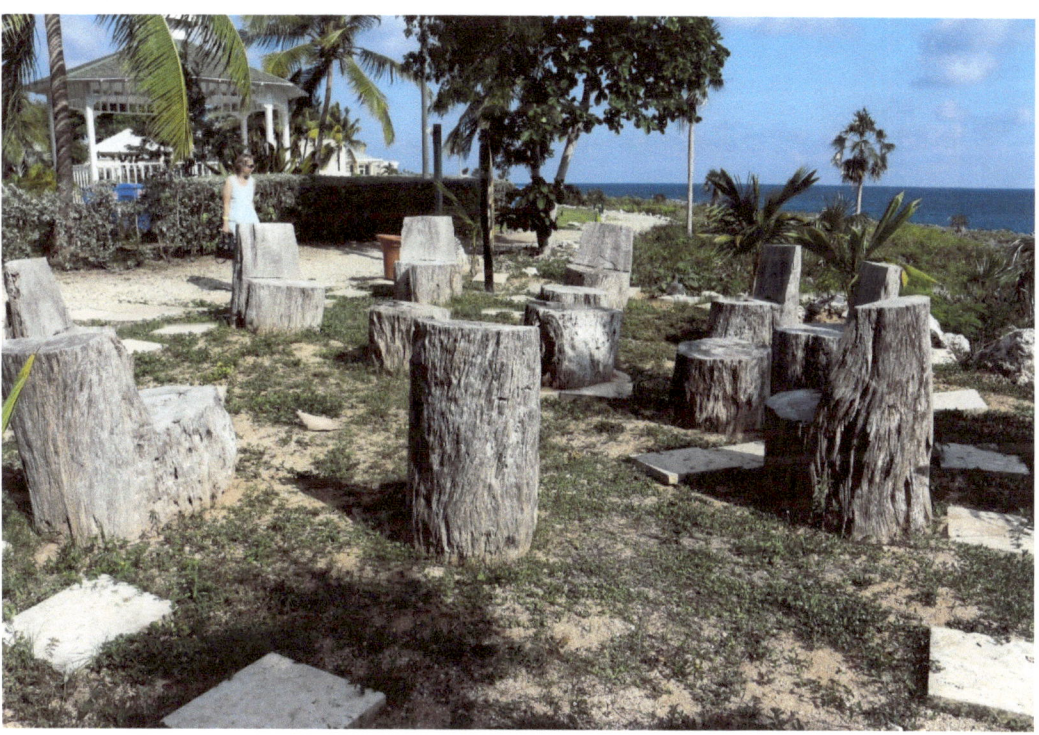

Garden – Pedro St. James

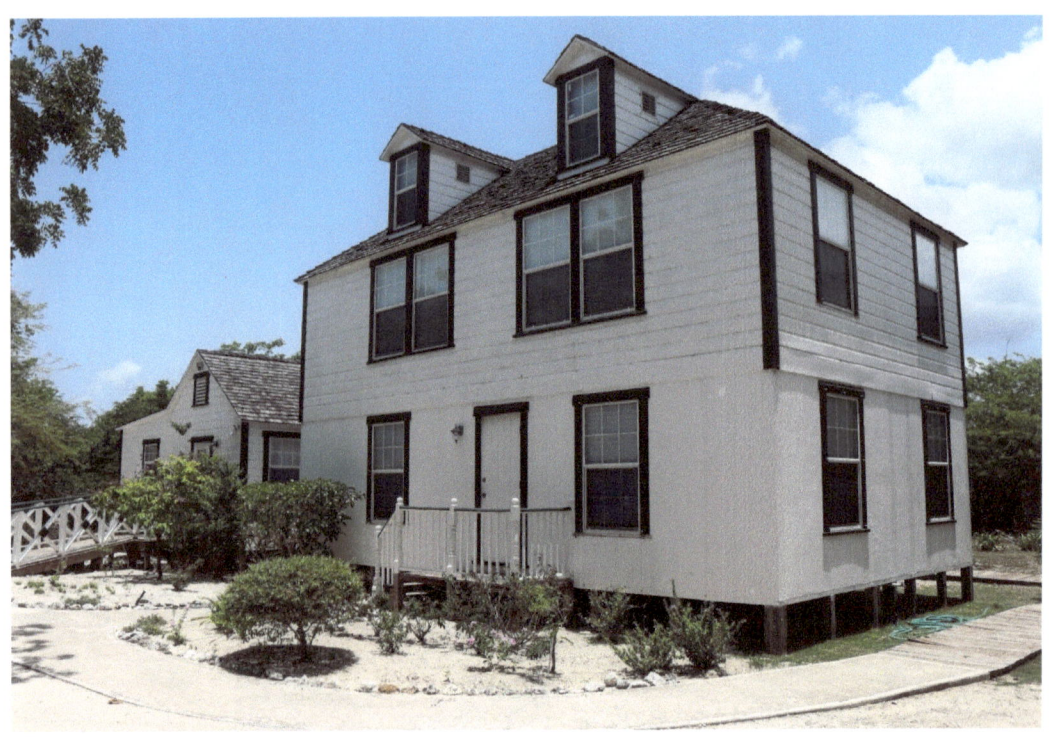

Mission House – Bodden Town

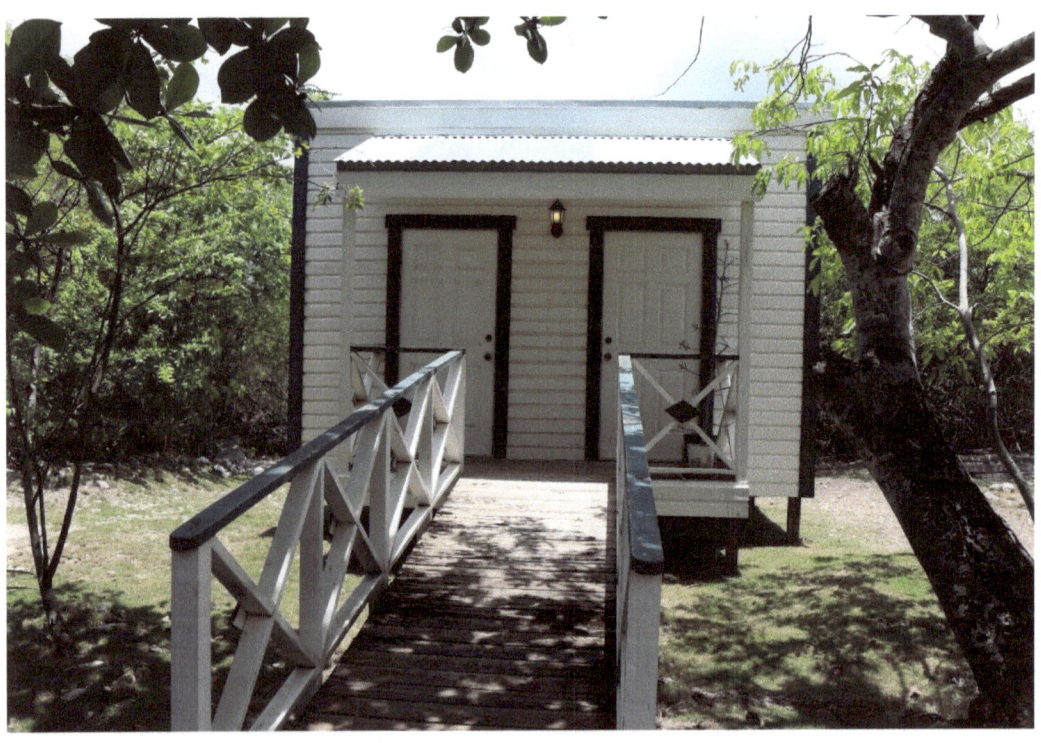

Mission House – Bodden Town

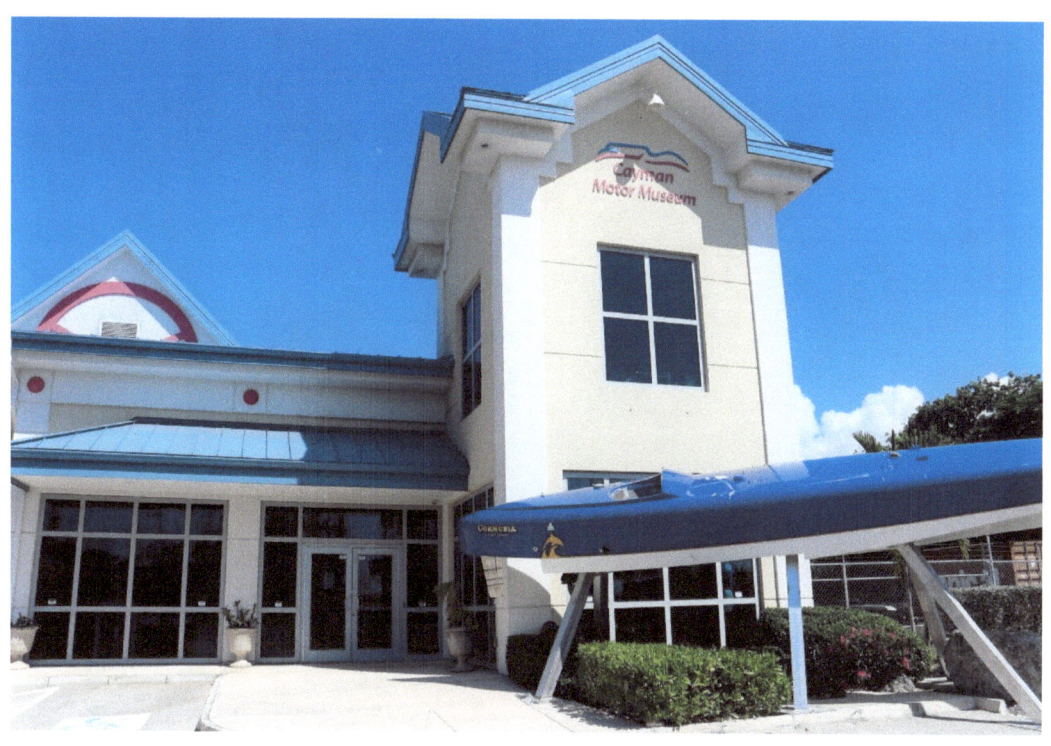

Motor Museum – West Bay

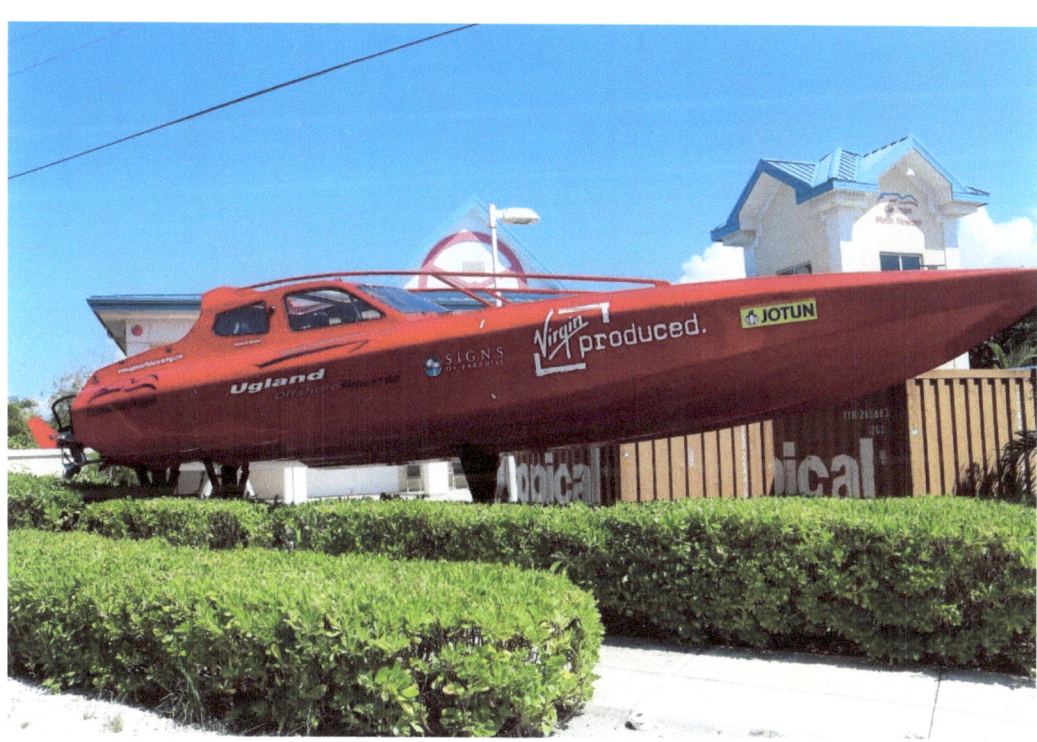

Motor Museum – West Bay

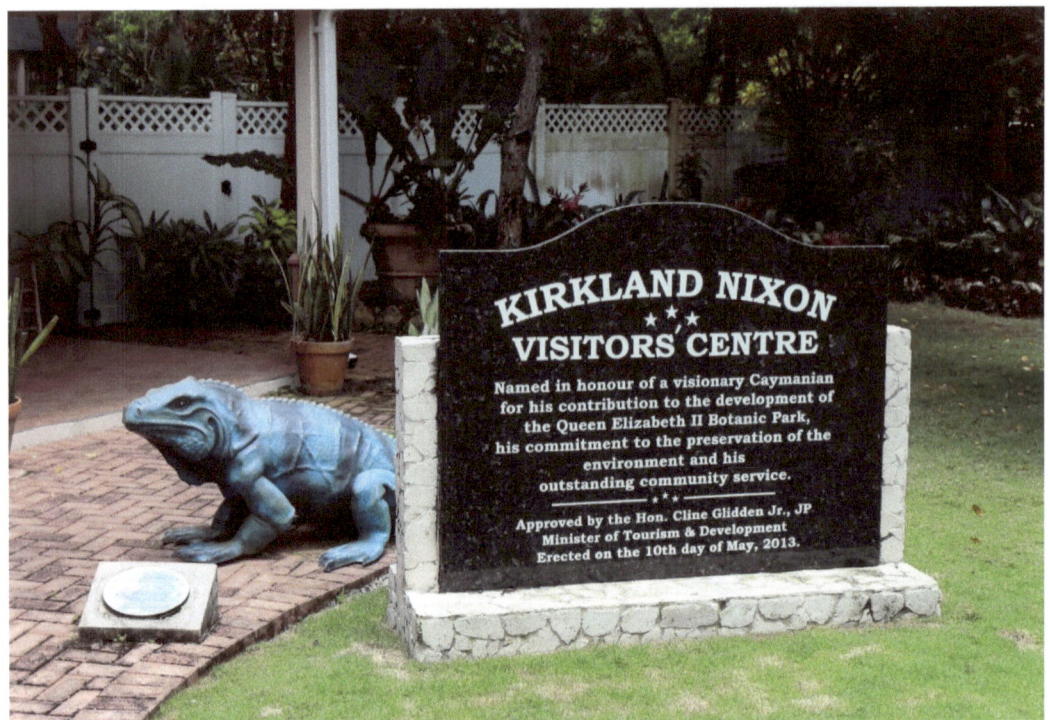

Queen Elizabeth II - Botanic Garden

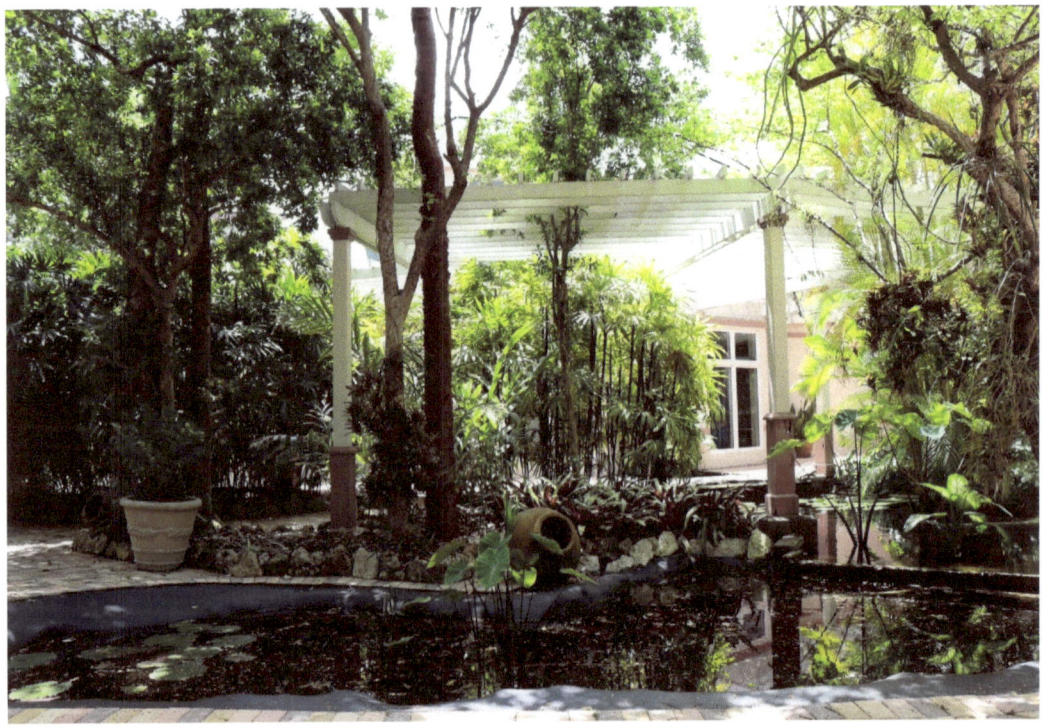

Botanic Garden – Garden Cafe

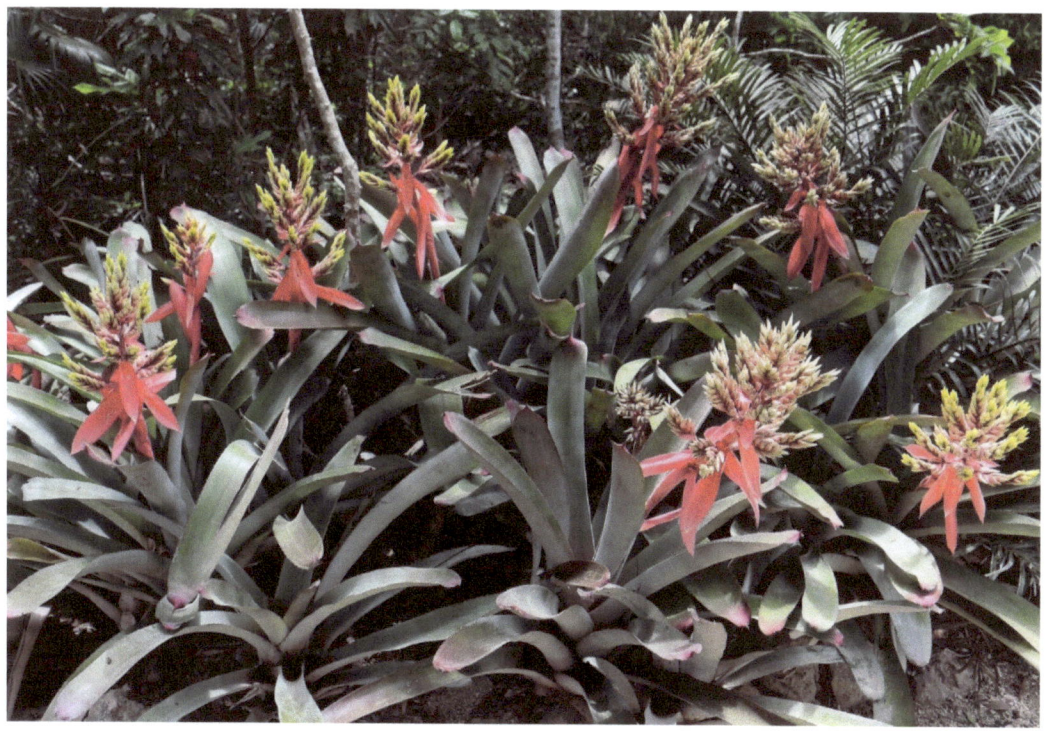

Botanic Garden

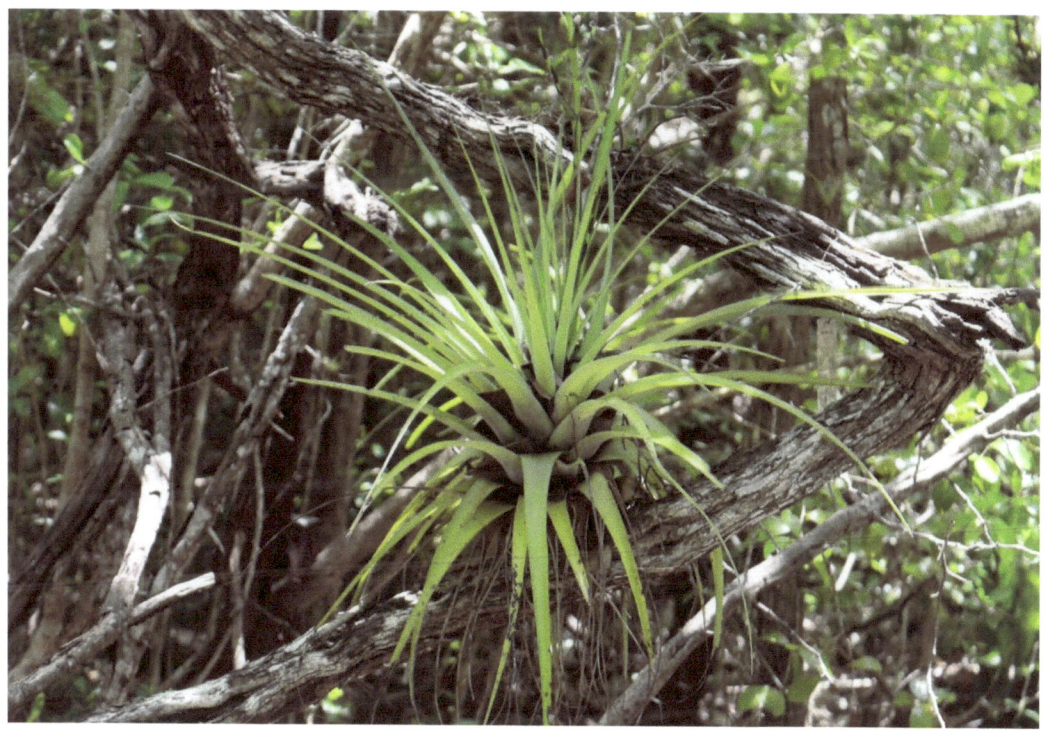

Botanic Garden - Orchid

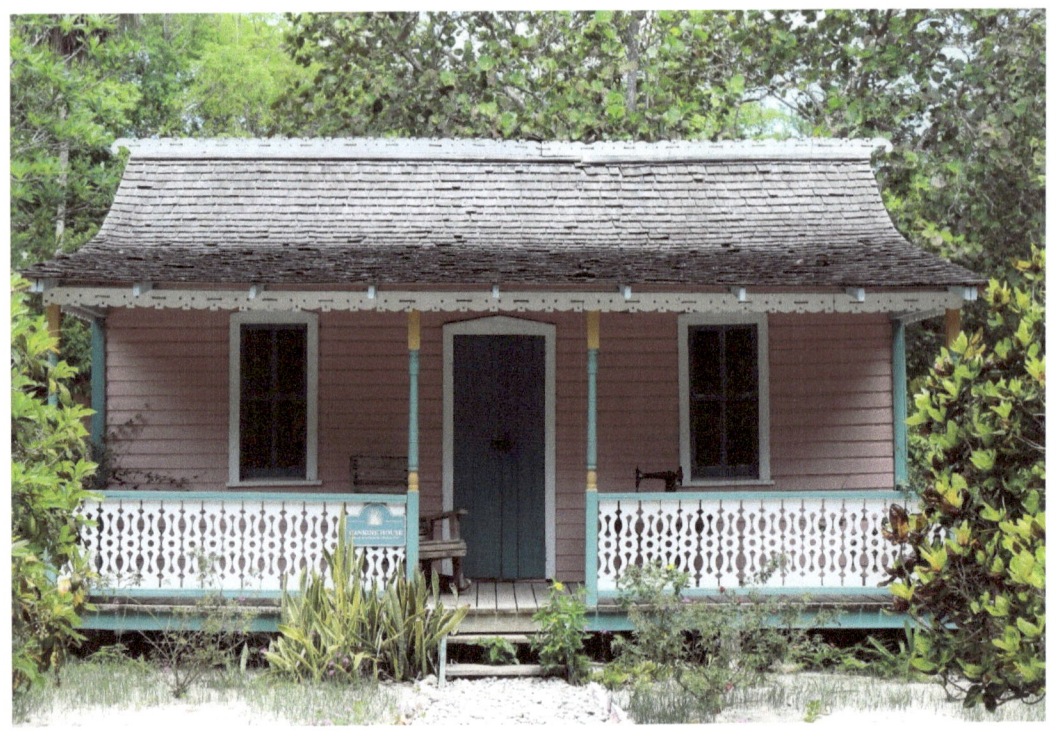

Botanic Garden – Traditional Cayman House

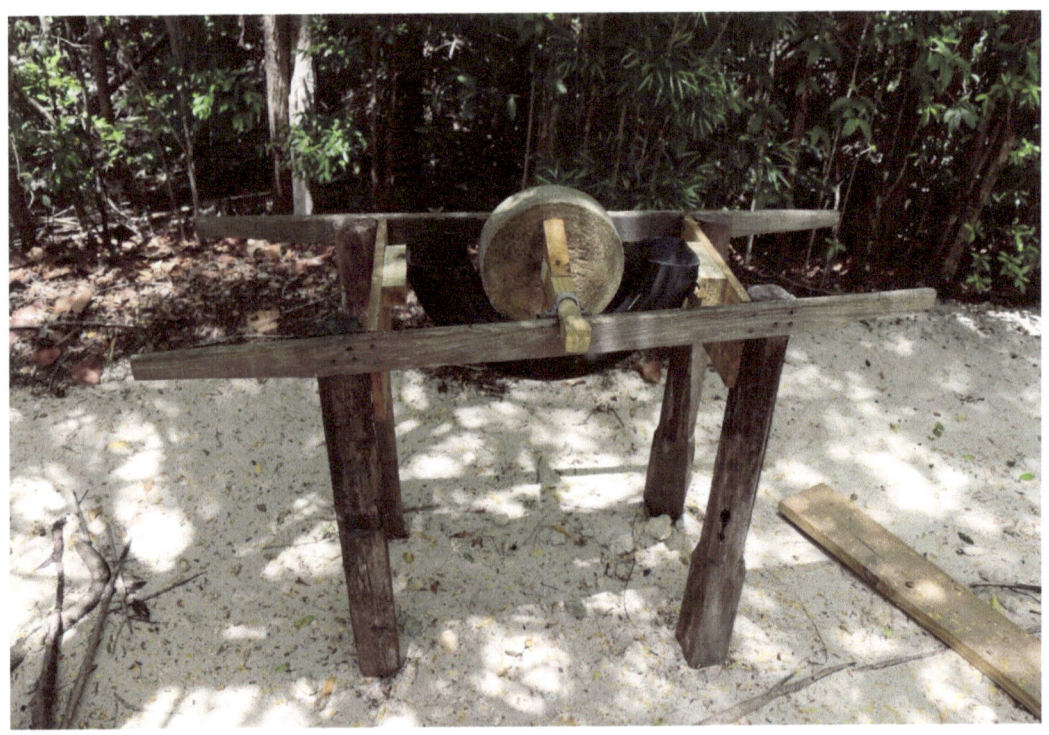

Botanic Garden – Knife Sharpener

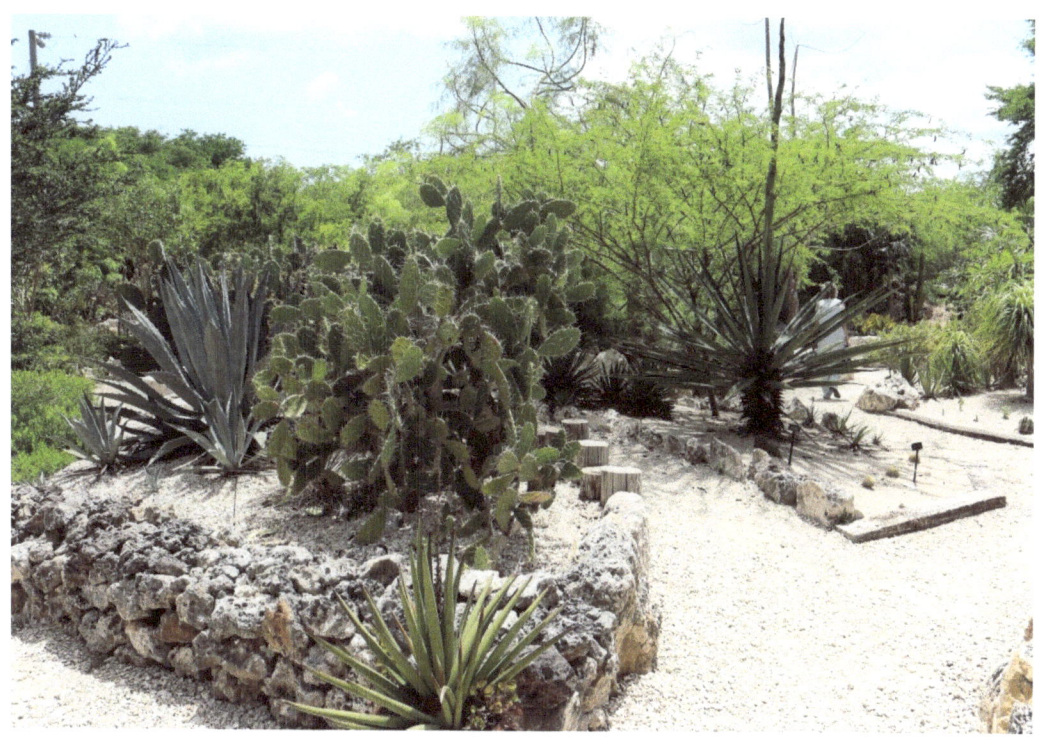

Botanic Garden – Medicine Garden

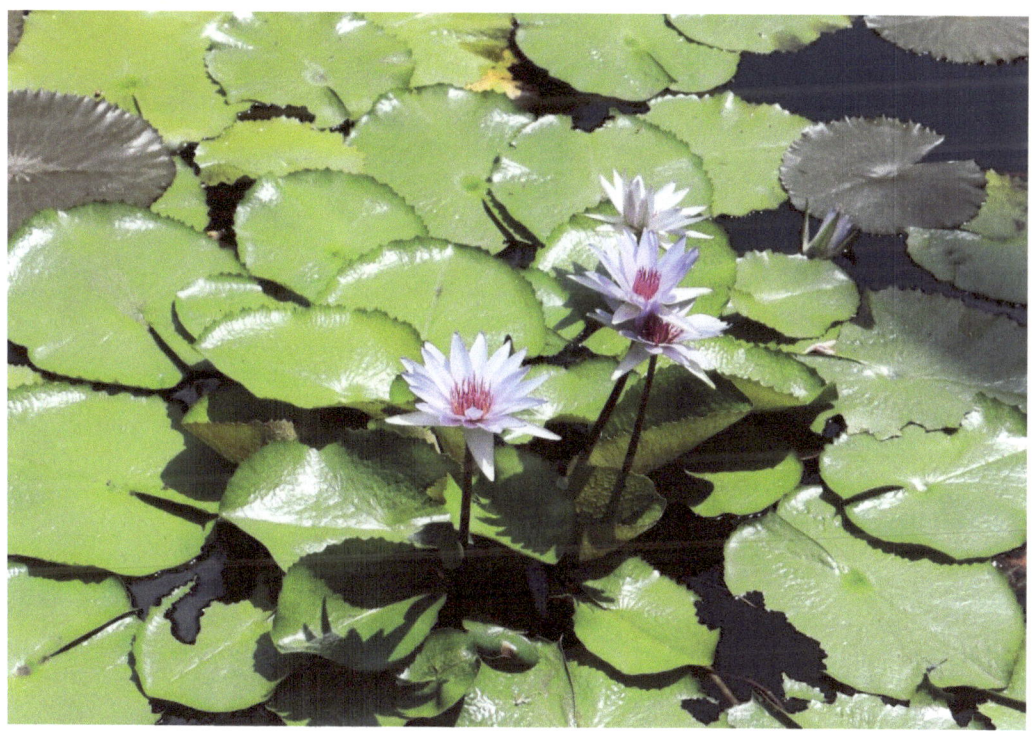

Botanic Garden – Sea Roses at the Tea Pavilion

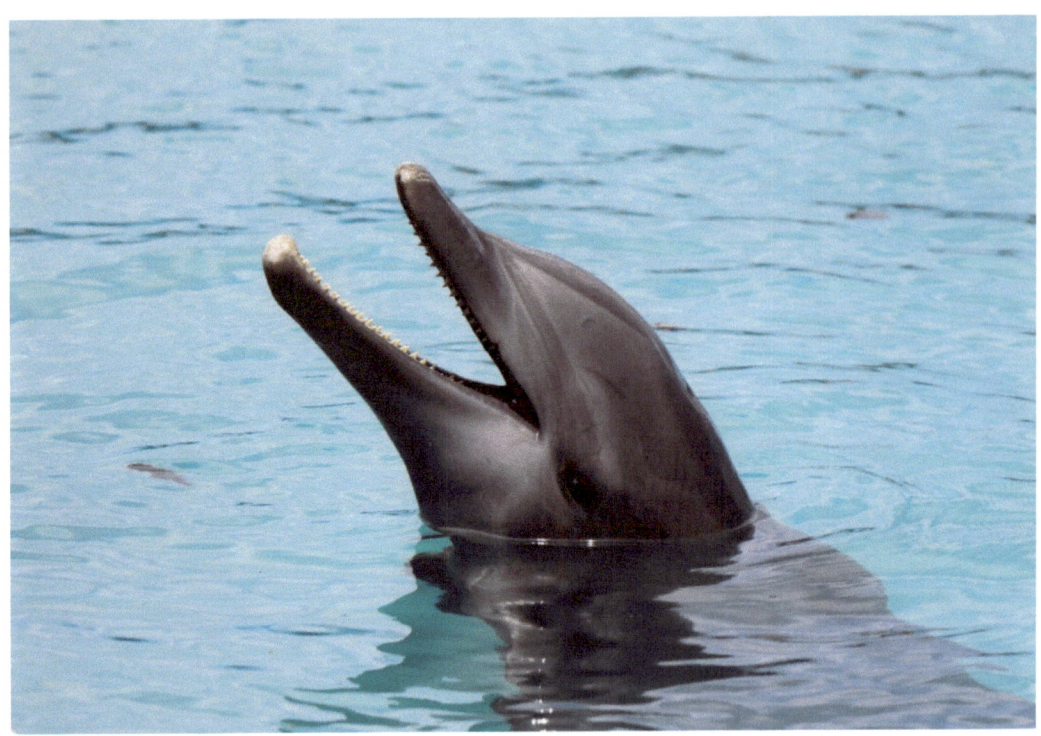

Dolphin in Dolphin Cove

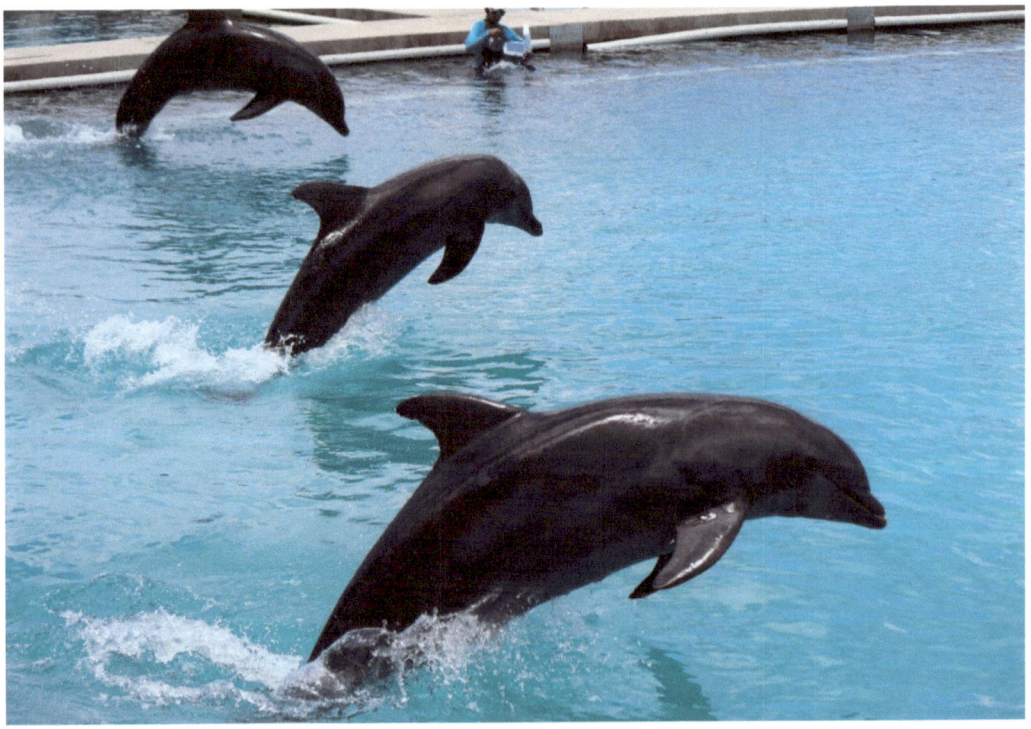

Dolphin Dance in Dolphin Cove

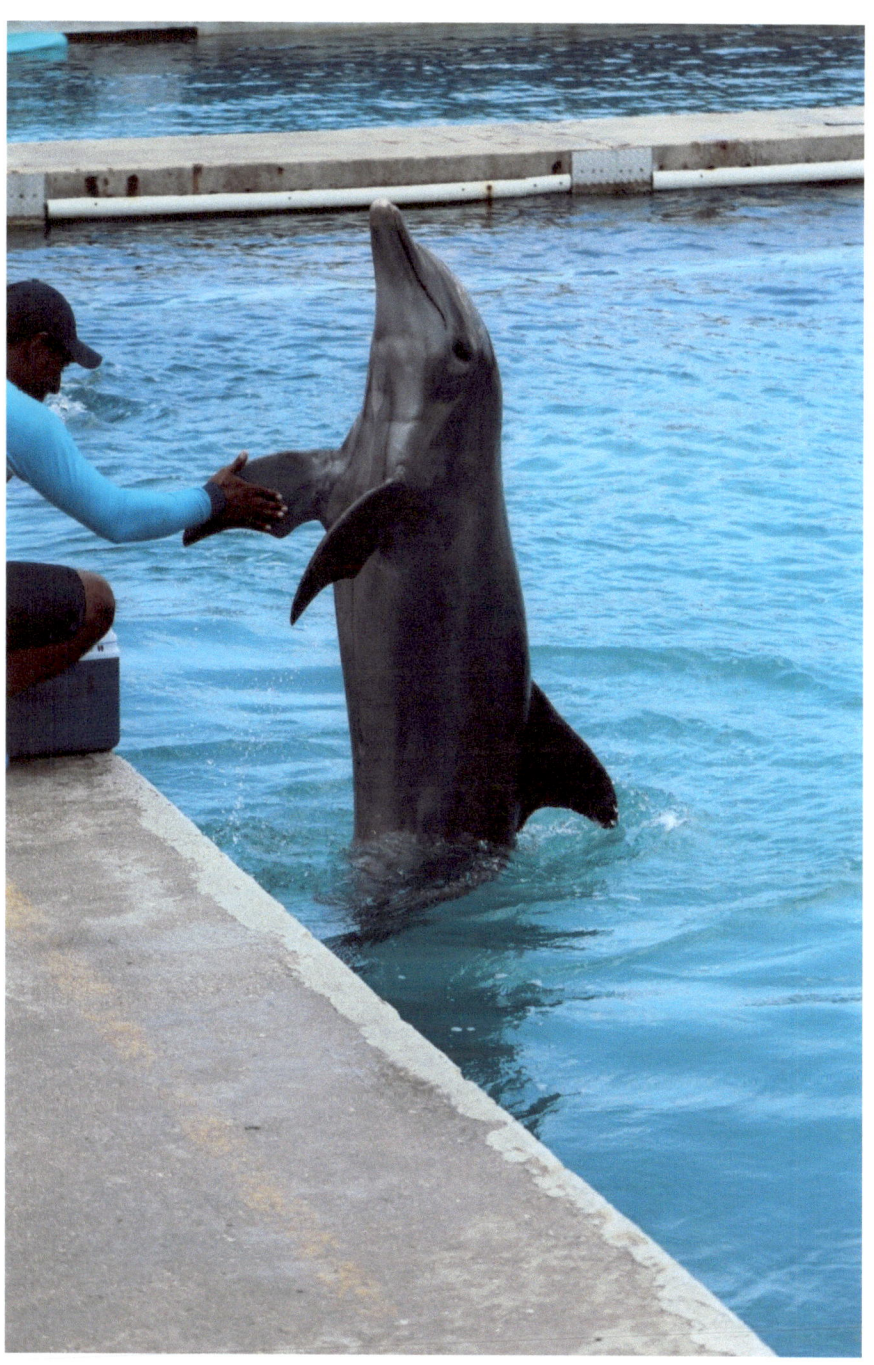

Give me Five - the Dolphin Way

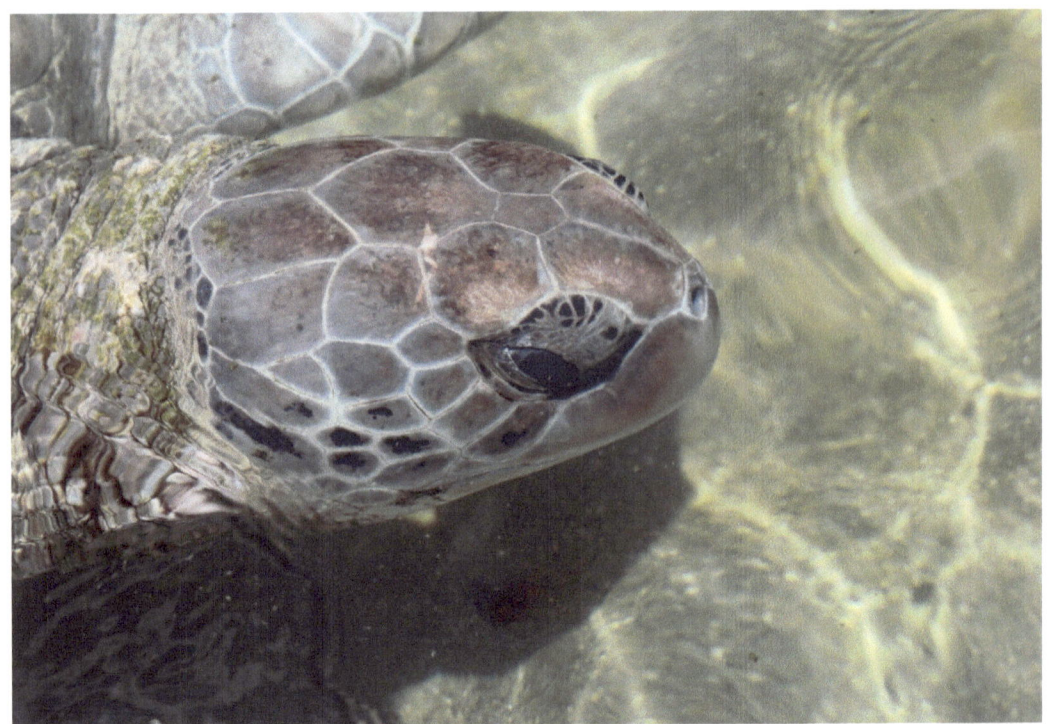

Green Sea Turtle

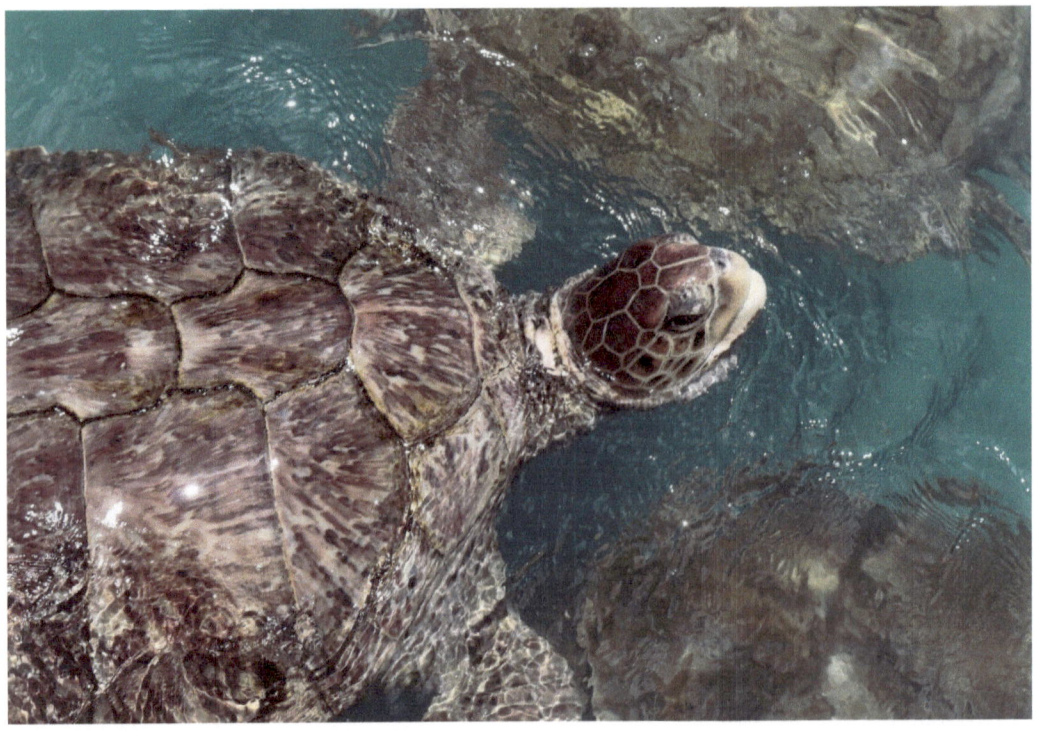

Green Sea Turtle in the Breeding Pond

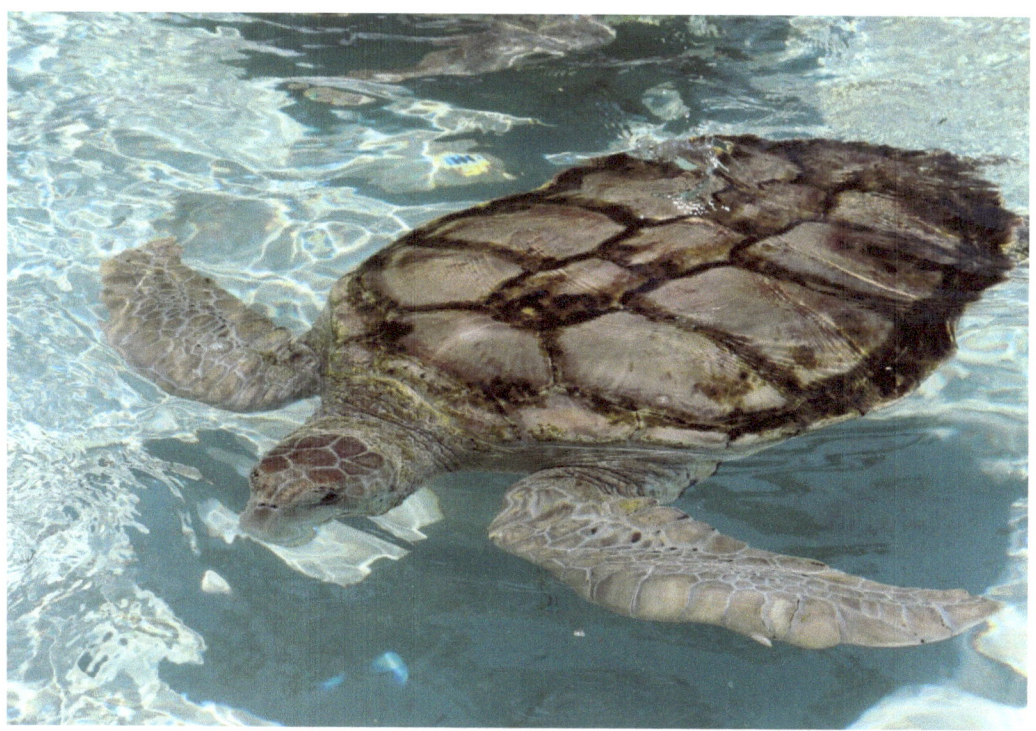

Sea Turtle in the Petting Pond

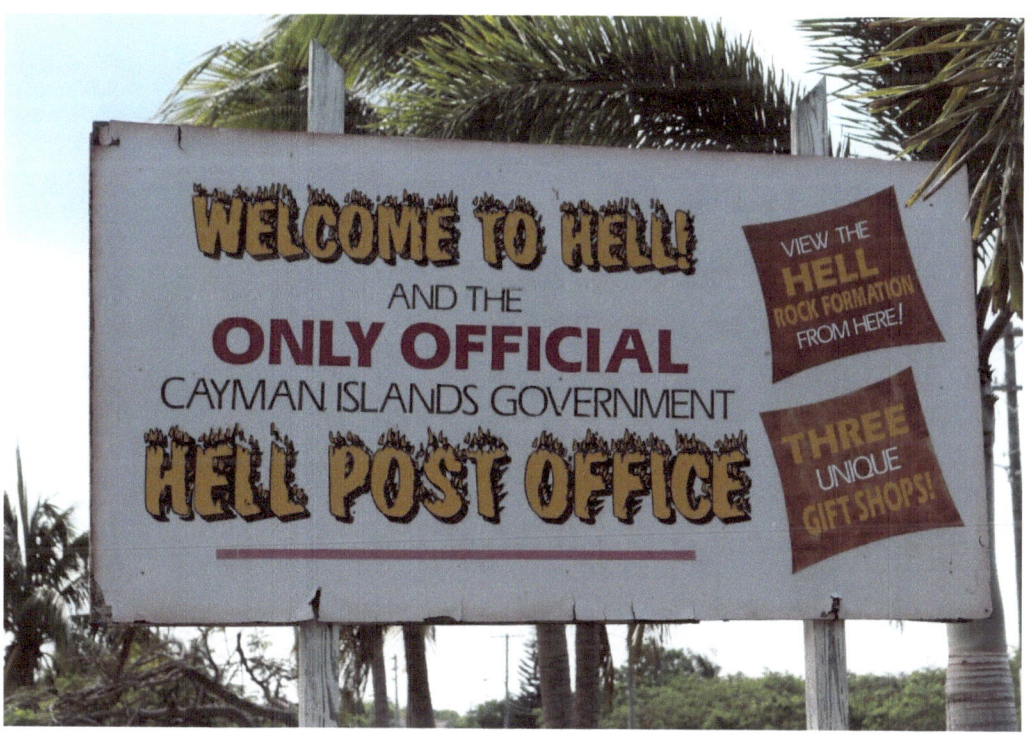

Want to send a Post Card from Hell?

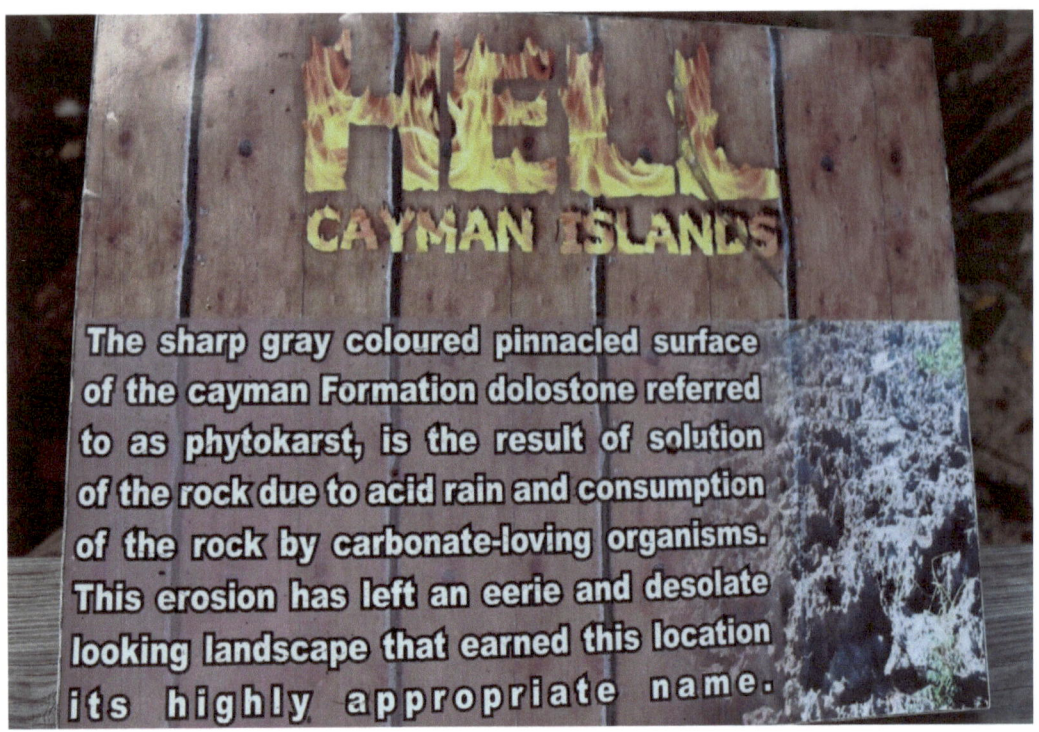

The sharp gray coloured pinnacled surface of the cayman Formation dolostone referred to as phytokarst, is the result of solution of the rock due to acid rain and consumption of the rock by carbonate-loving organisms. This erosion has left an eerie and desolate looking landscape that earned this location its highly appropriate name.

The Hell on Grand Cayman

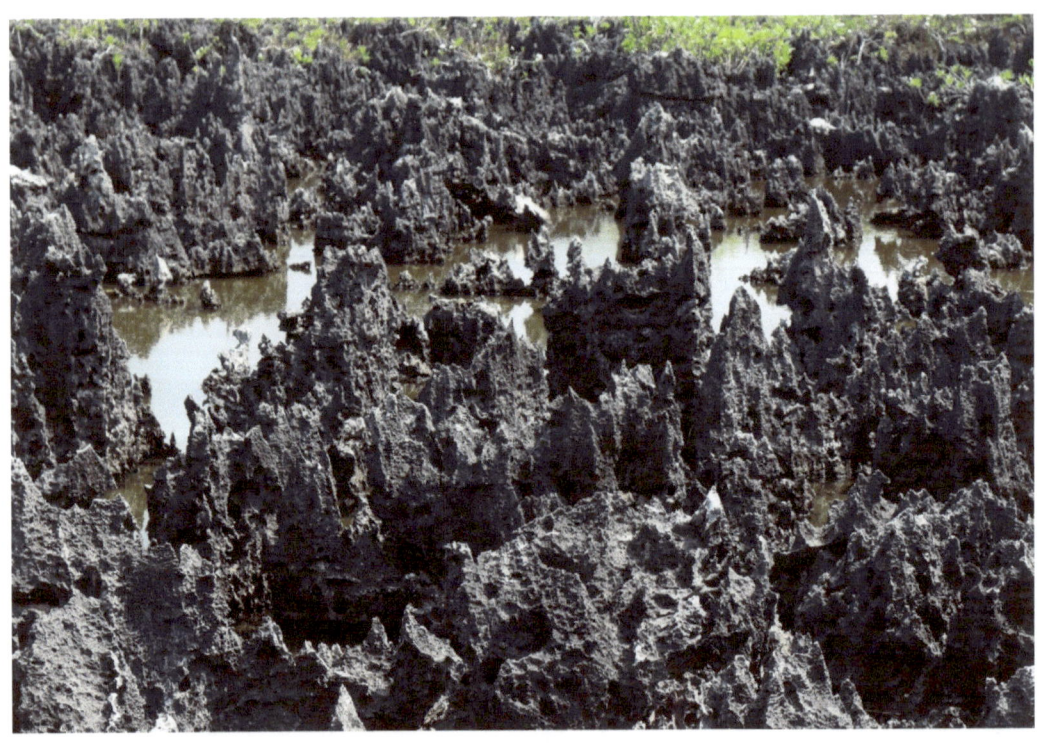

Looks like Hell!

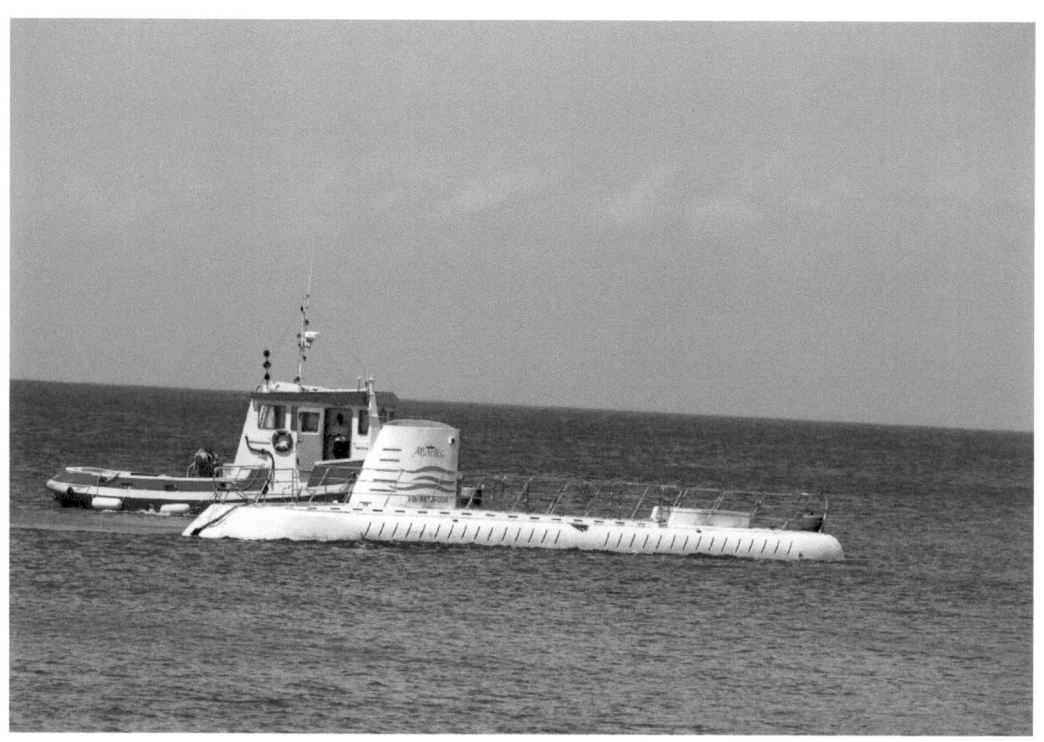

Let us go down with the White Submarine!

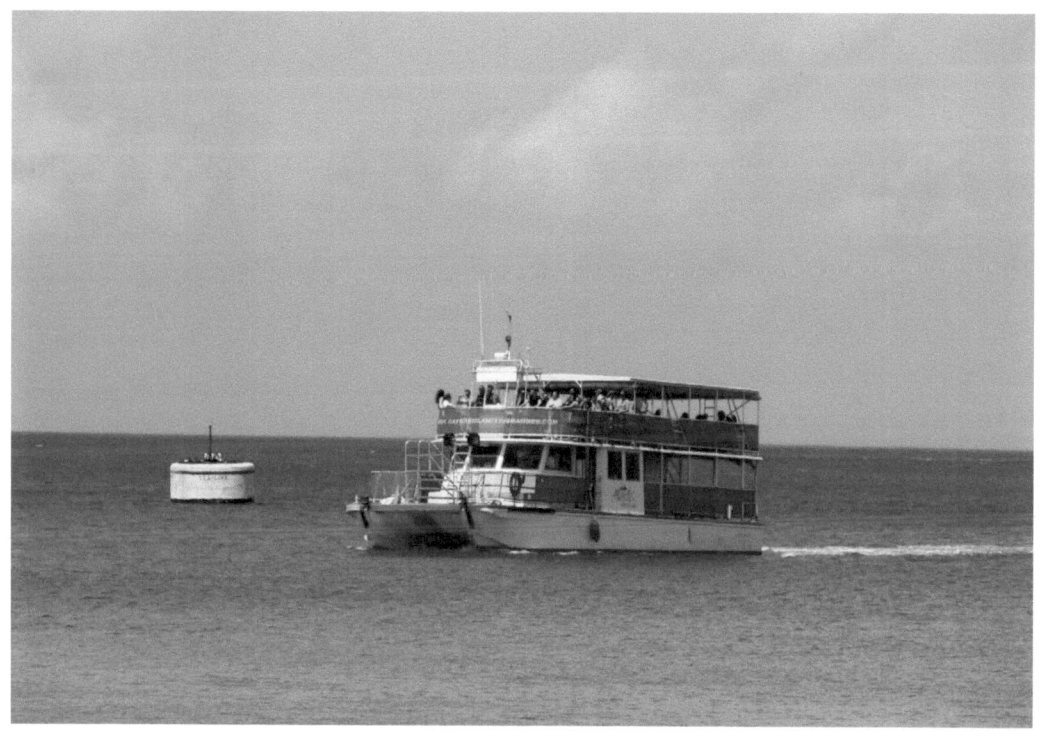

…or let us take the Glass Bottom Boat!

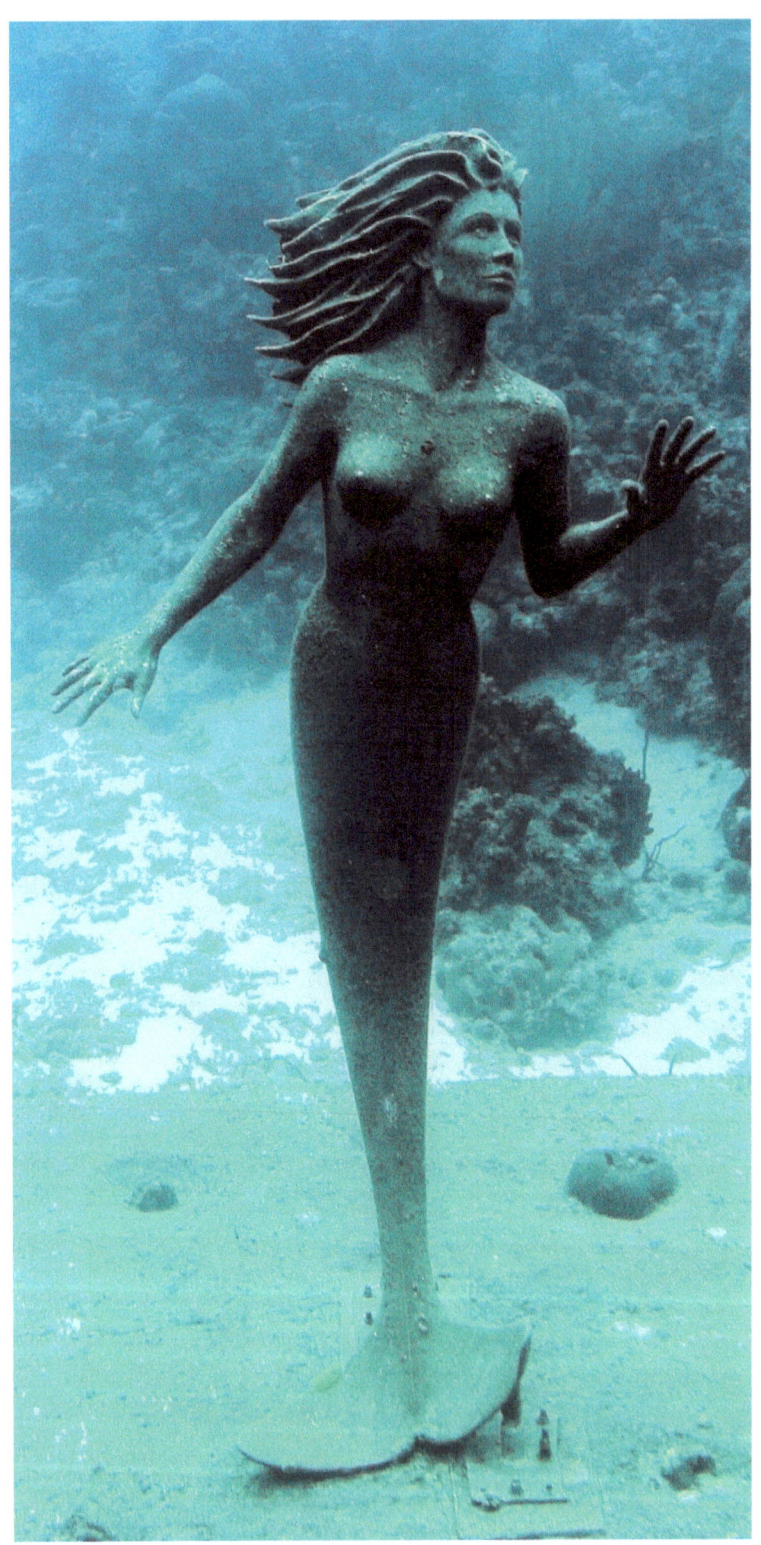

The Mermaid is calling for you!

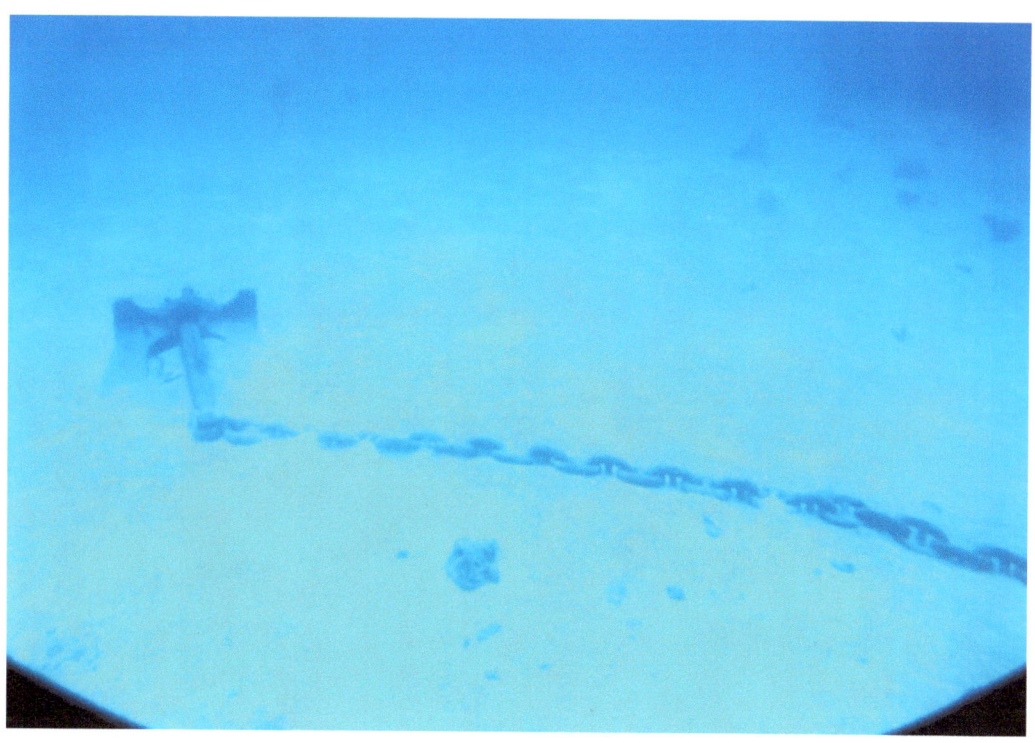

Impressions from under the Sea

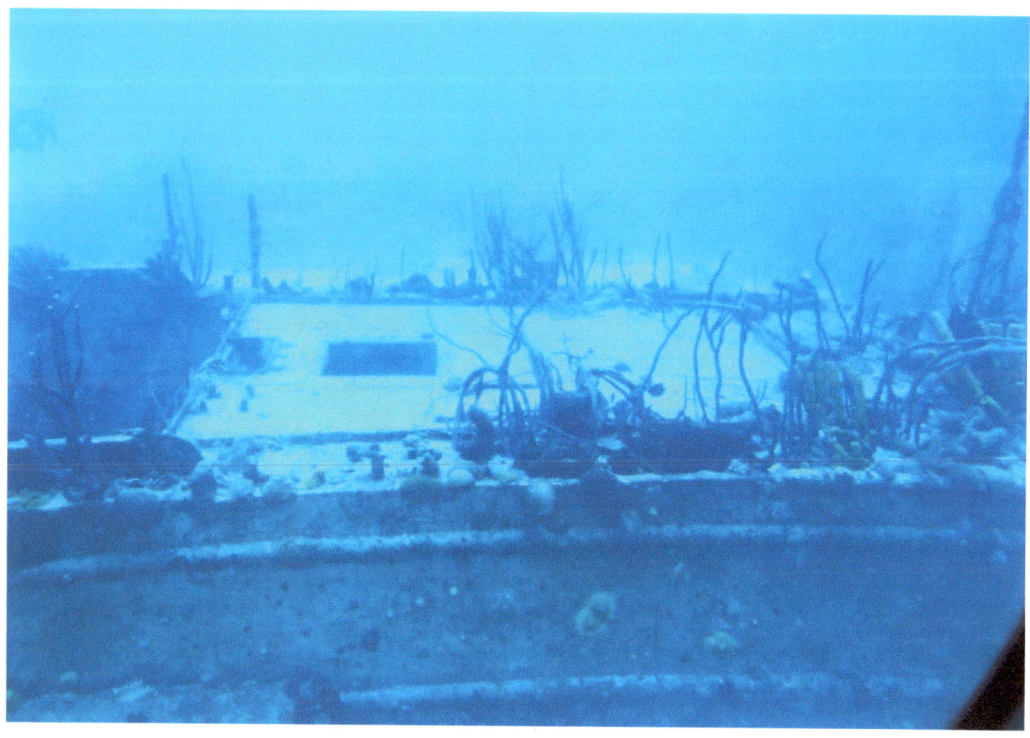

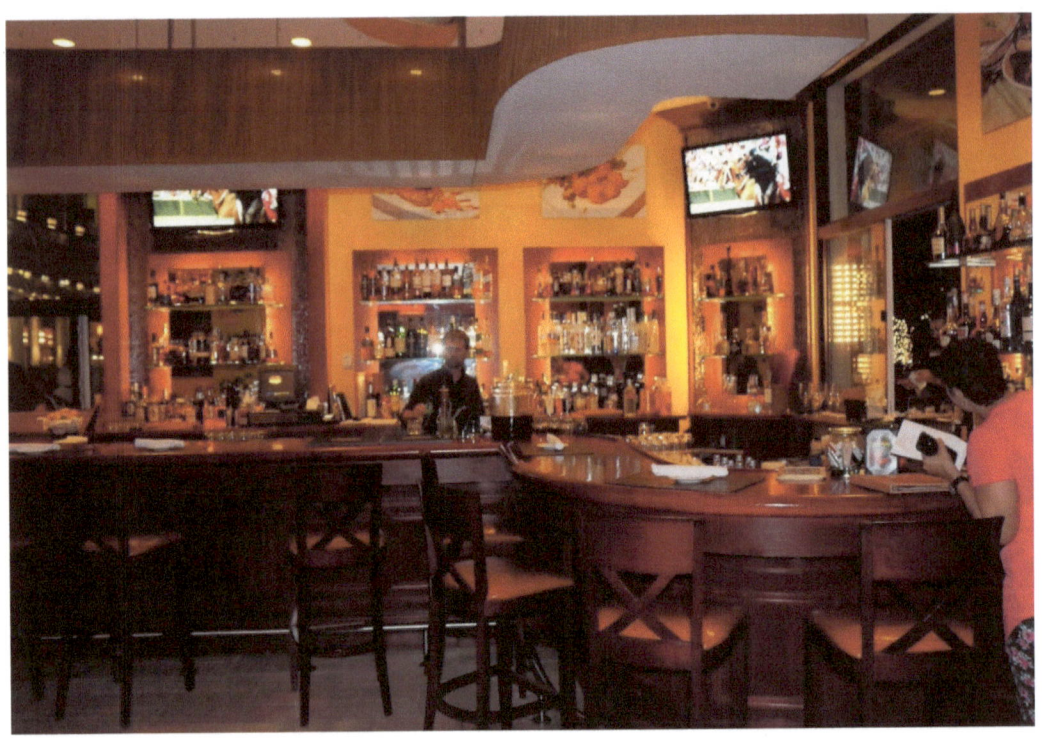

Many Restaurants wait for you

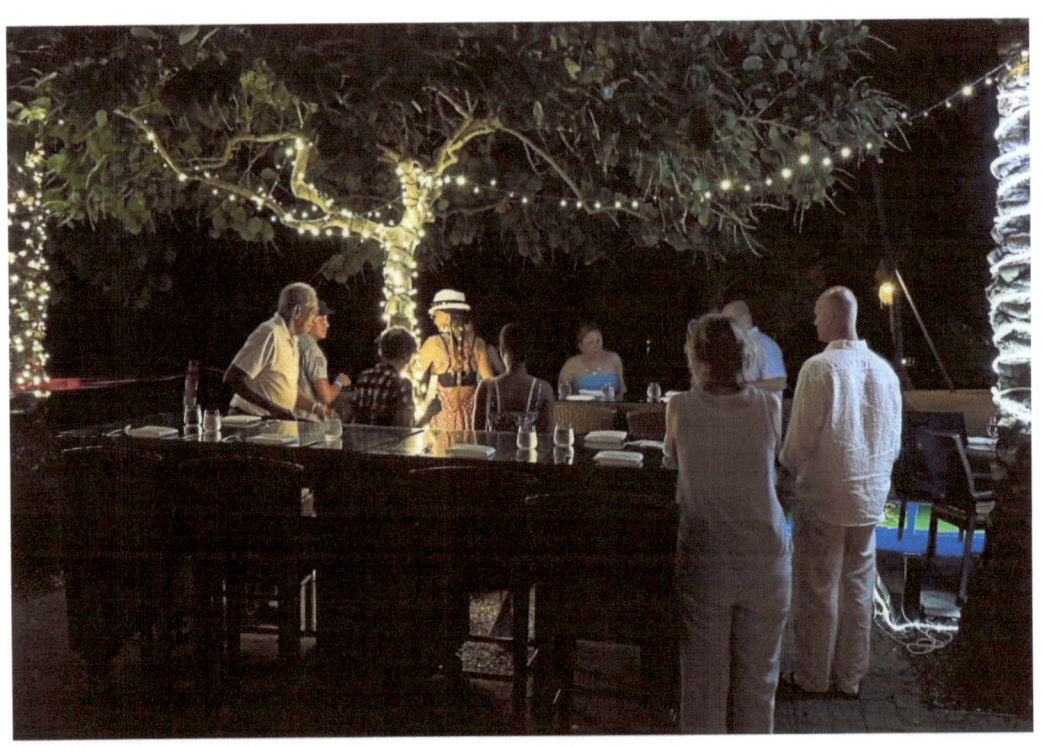

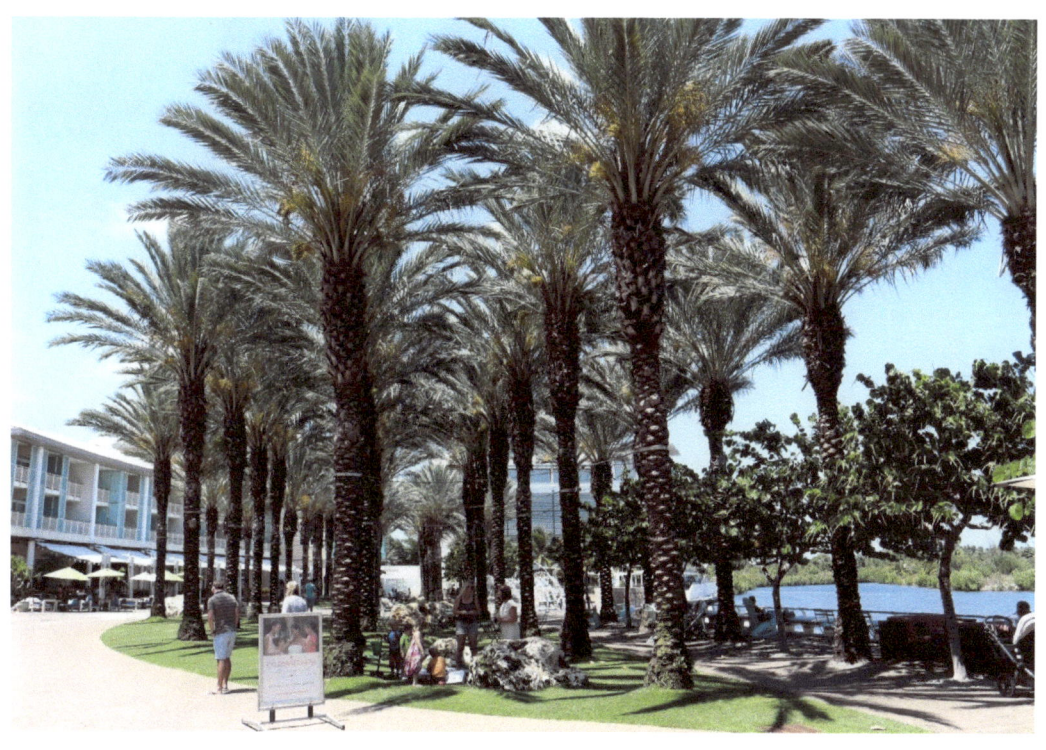

Camana Bay at daytime

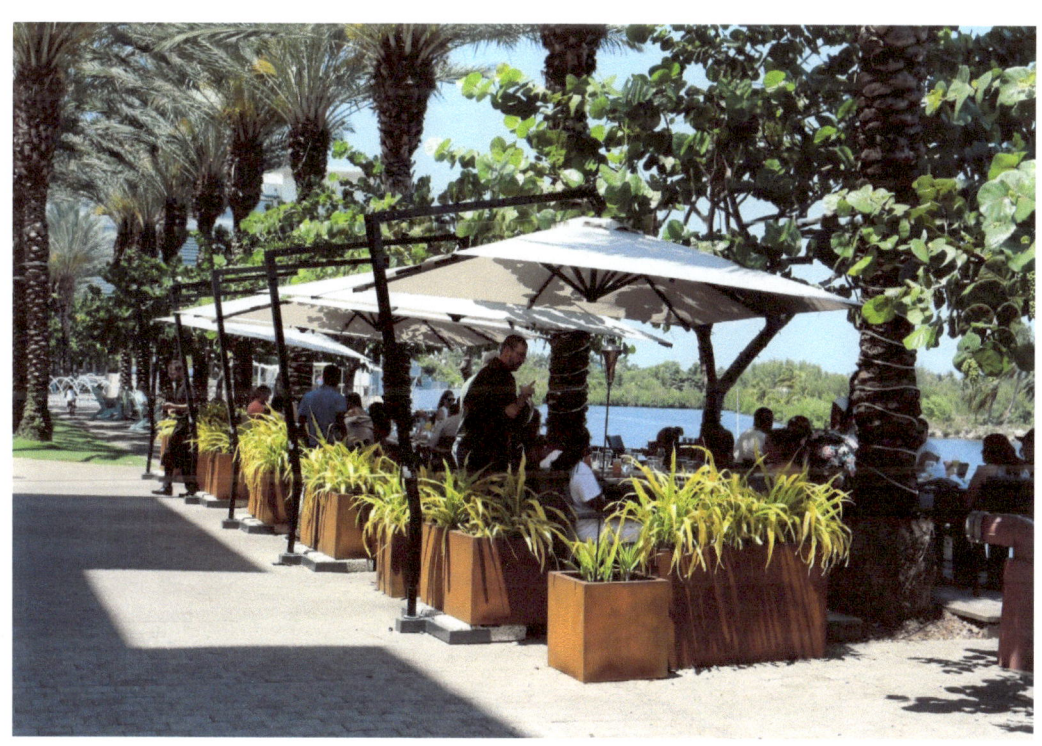

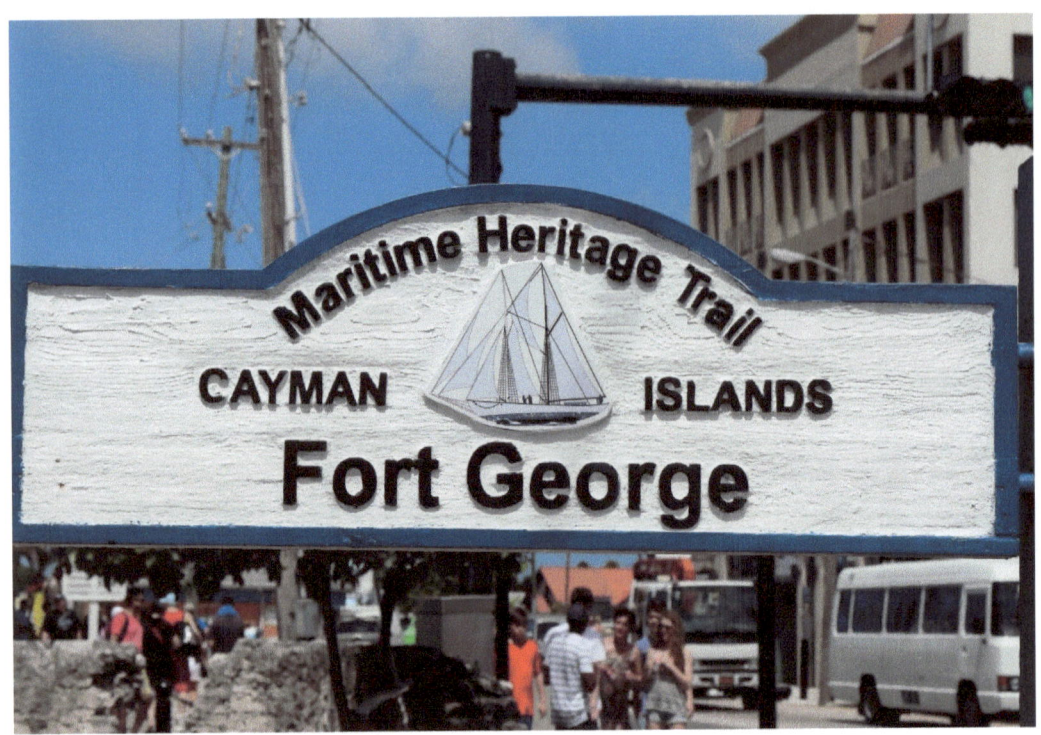

The Remains of the former Fort in Downtown Georgetown

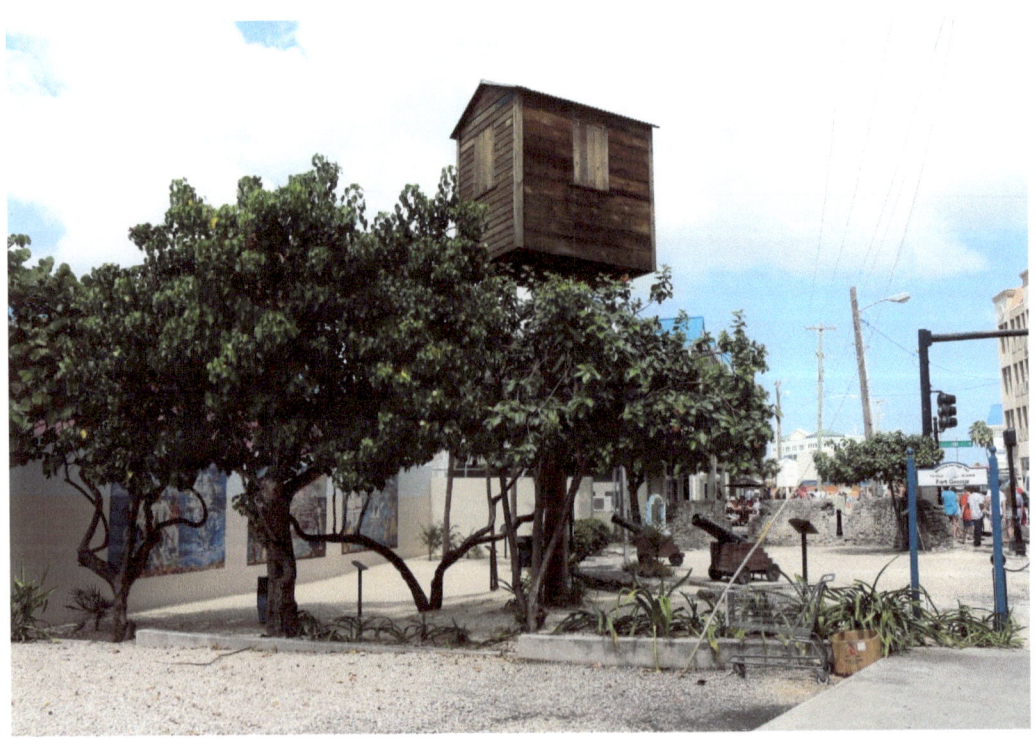

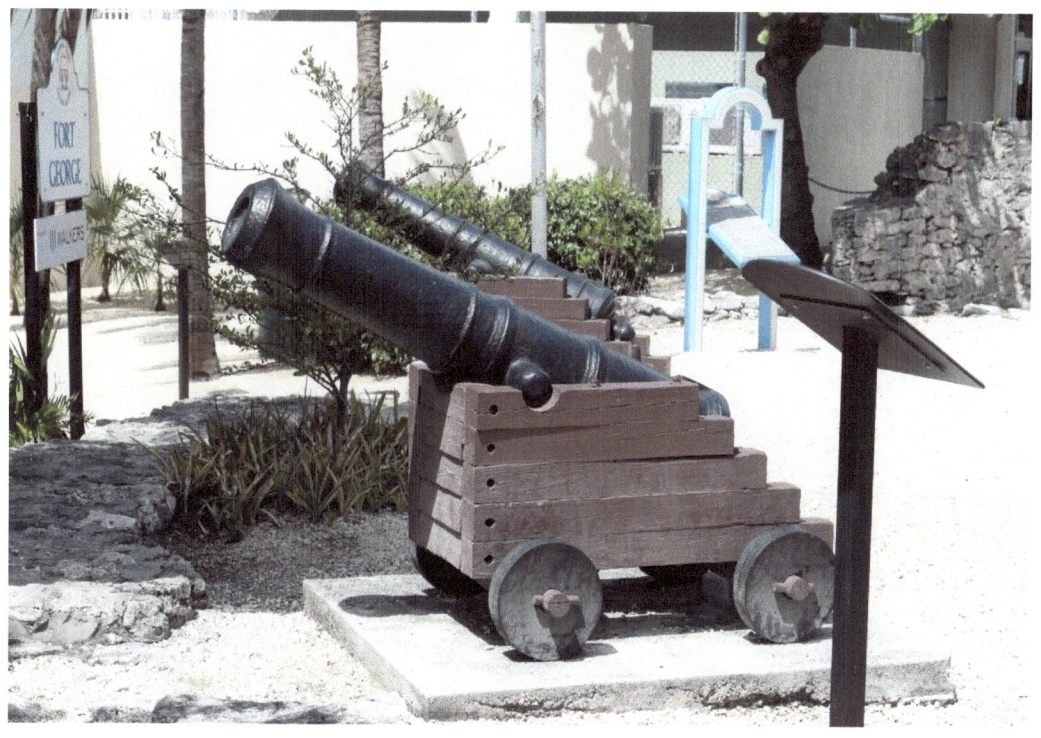

The National Museum at the Harbor with its Heritage exhibits from the Cayman Islands.

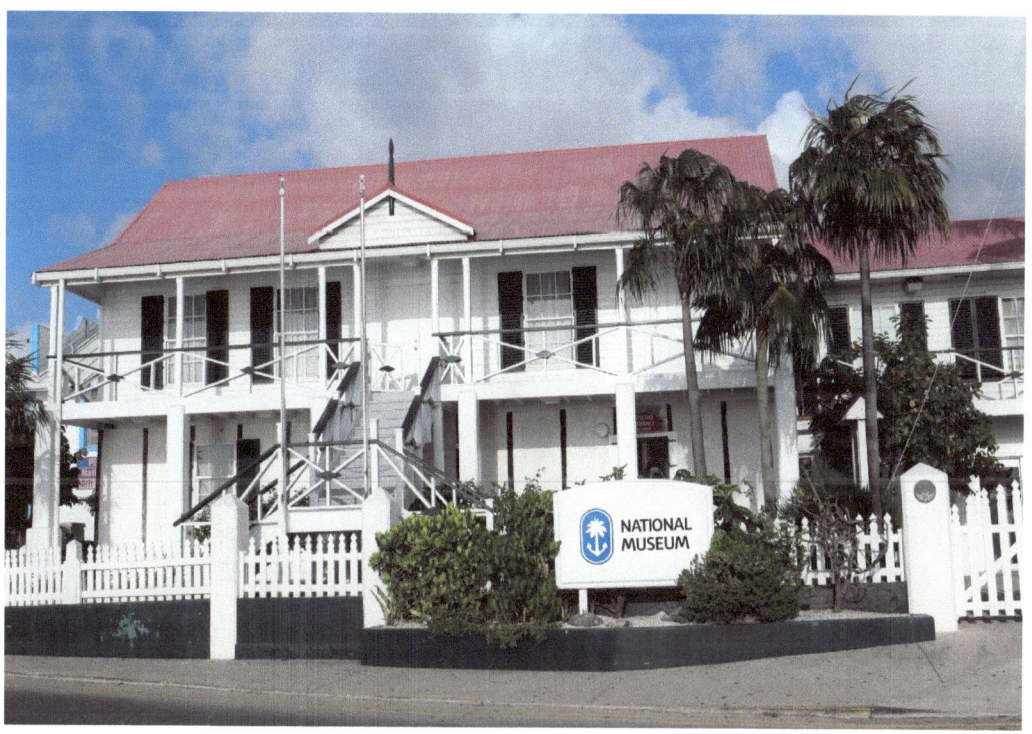

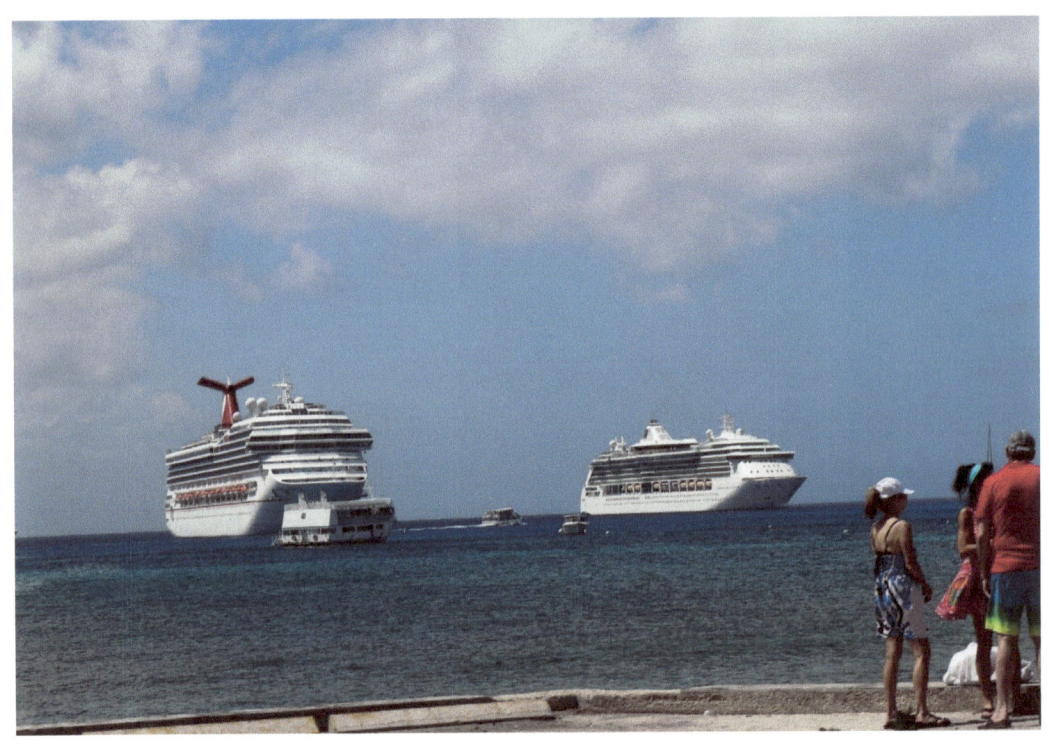

Harbor Impressions

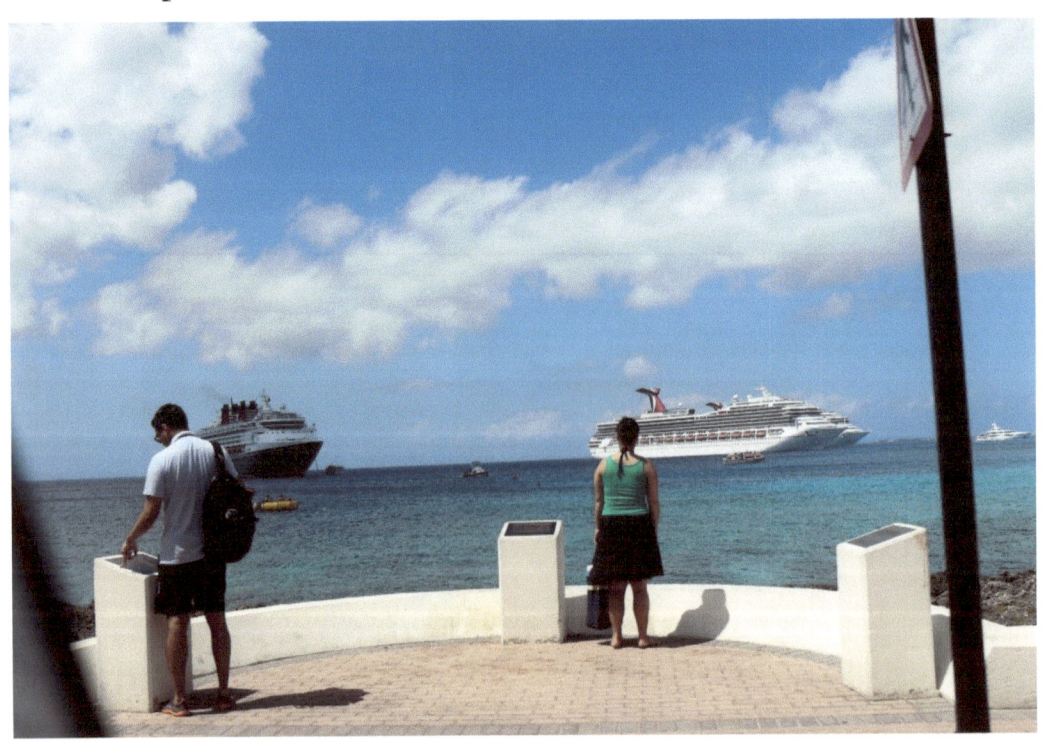

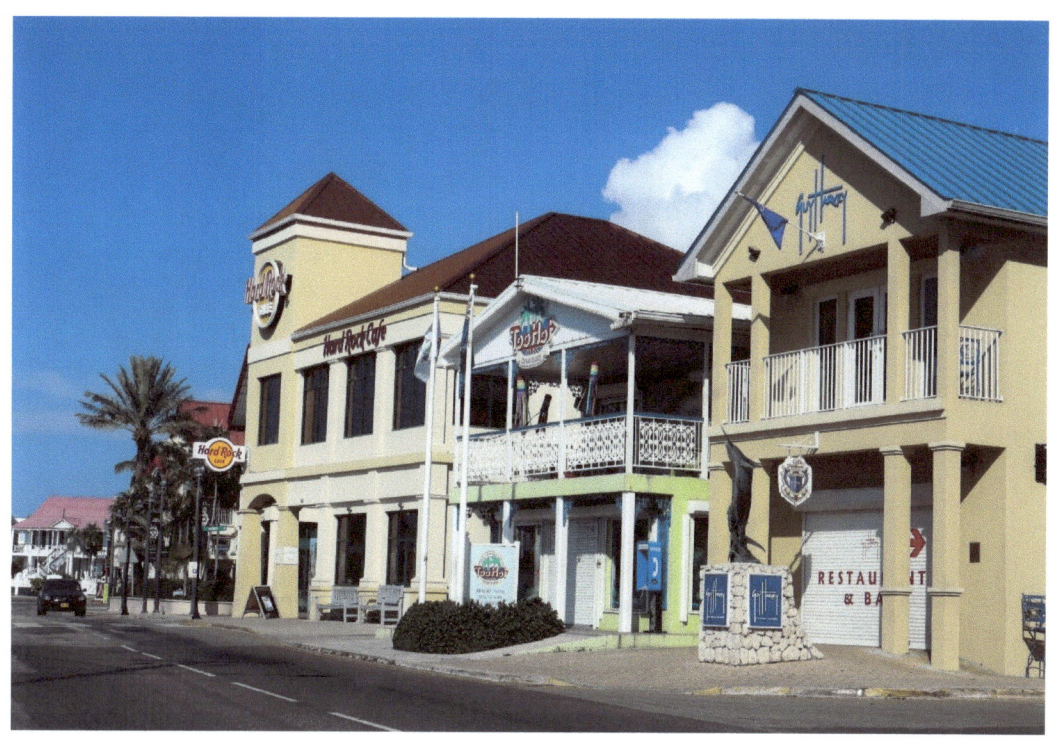

Shop until you drop – and all tax-free!

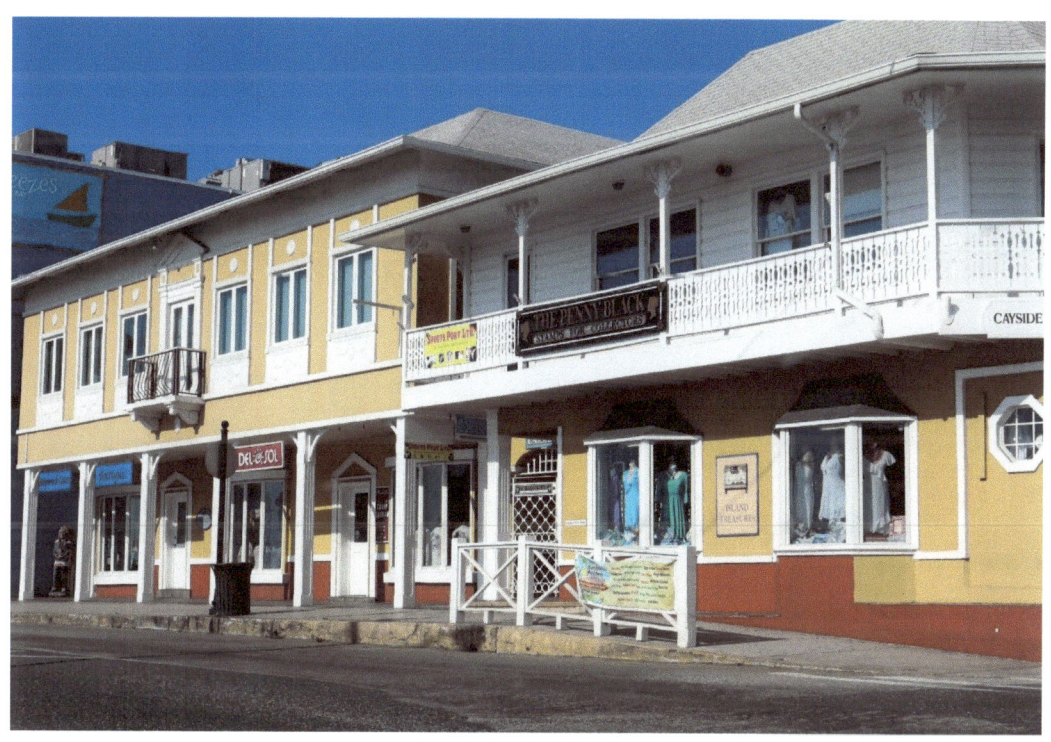

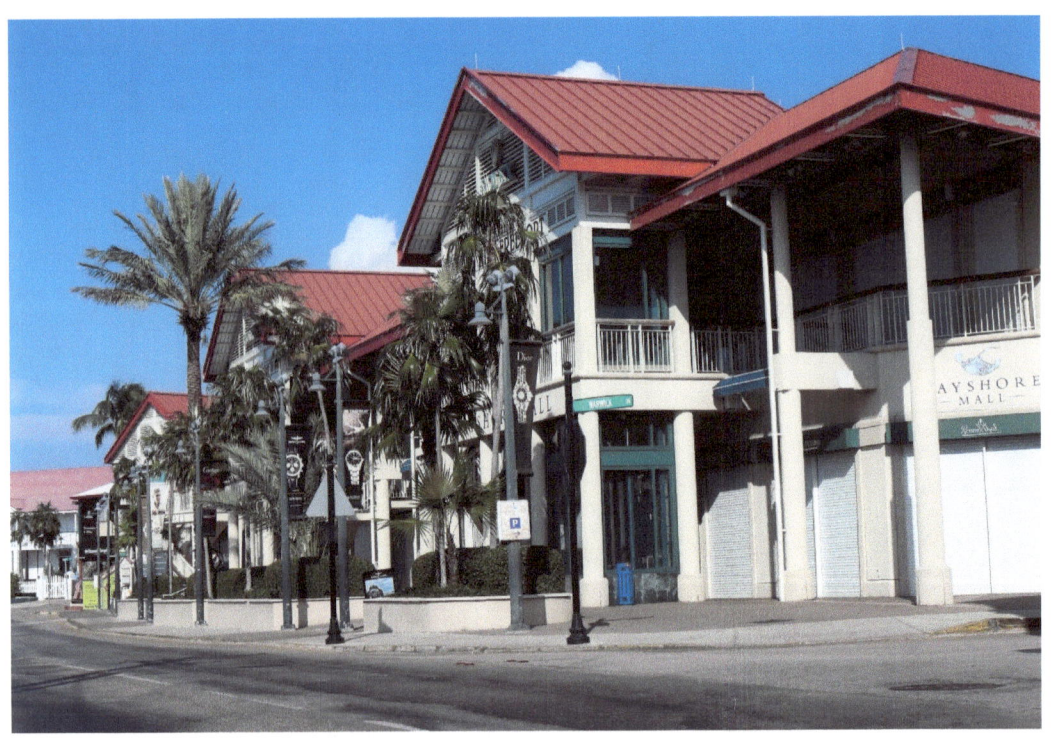

Shops and Restaurants – and all tax-free!

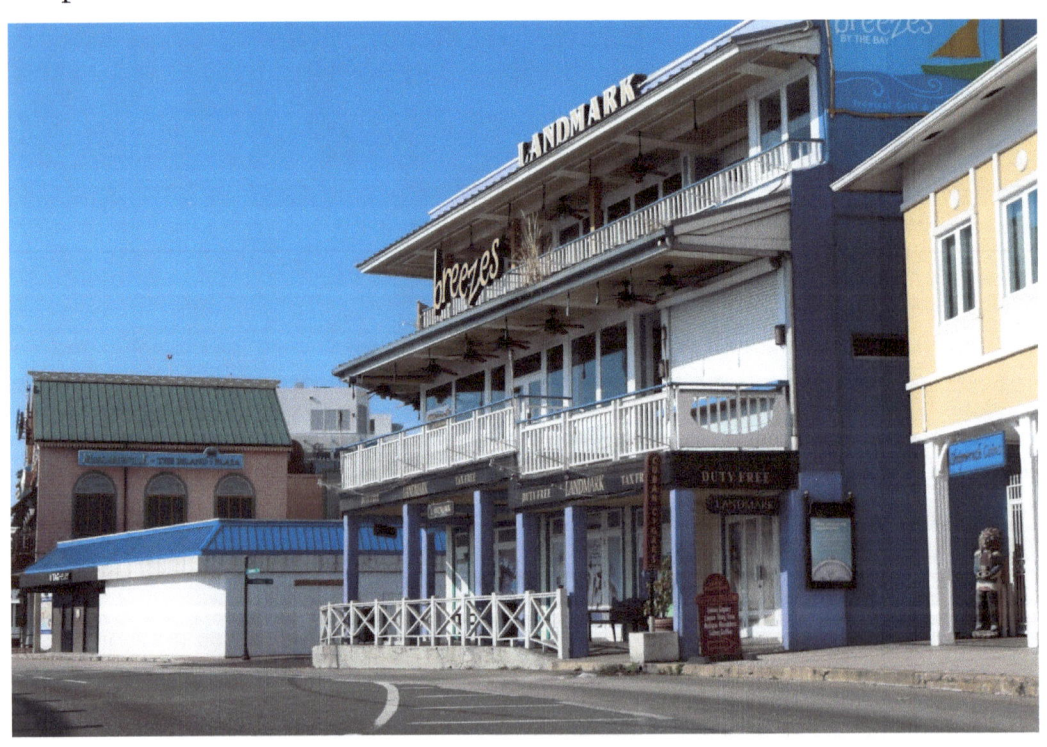

Art in the Downtown Area

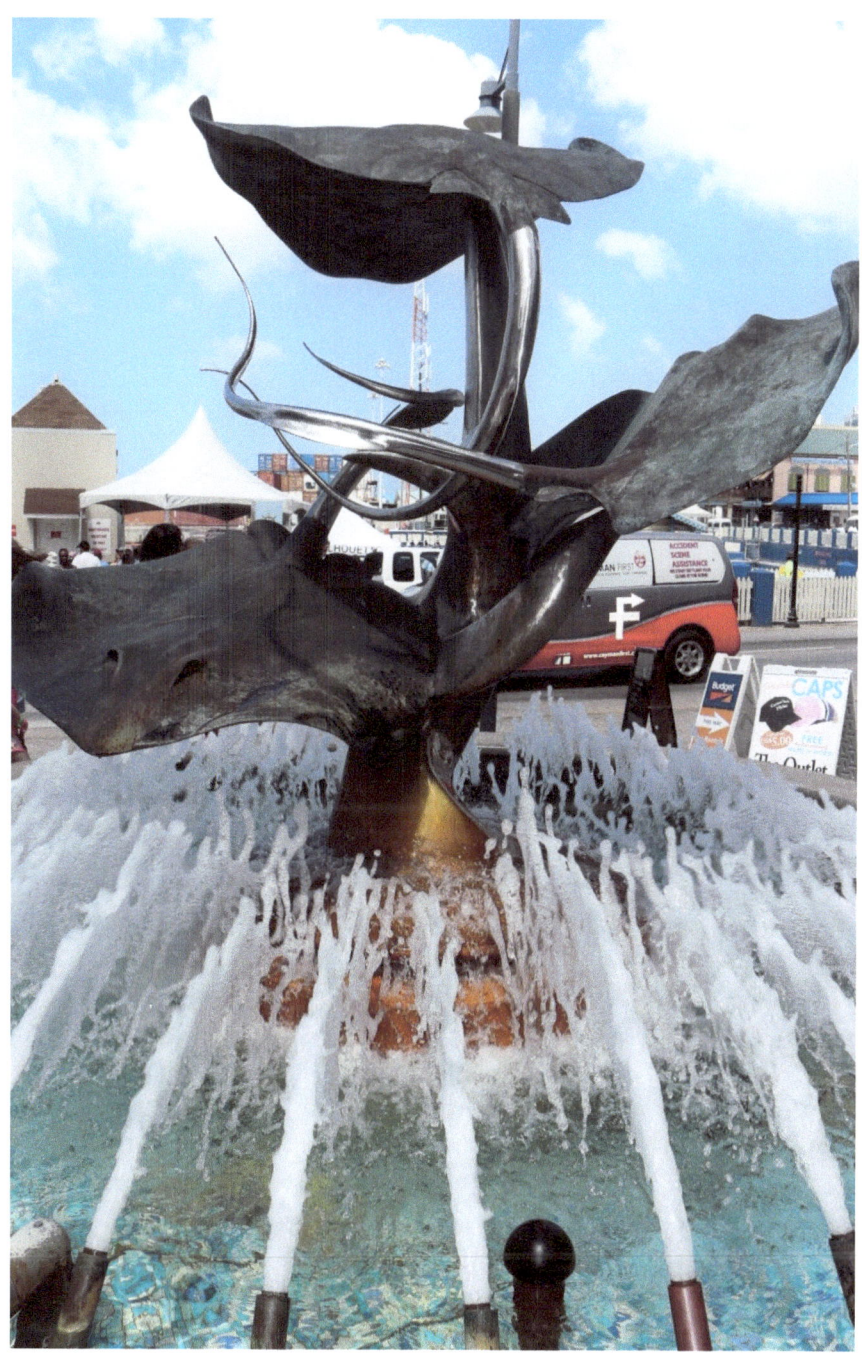

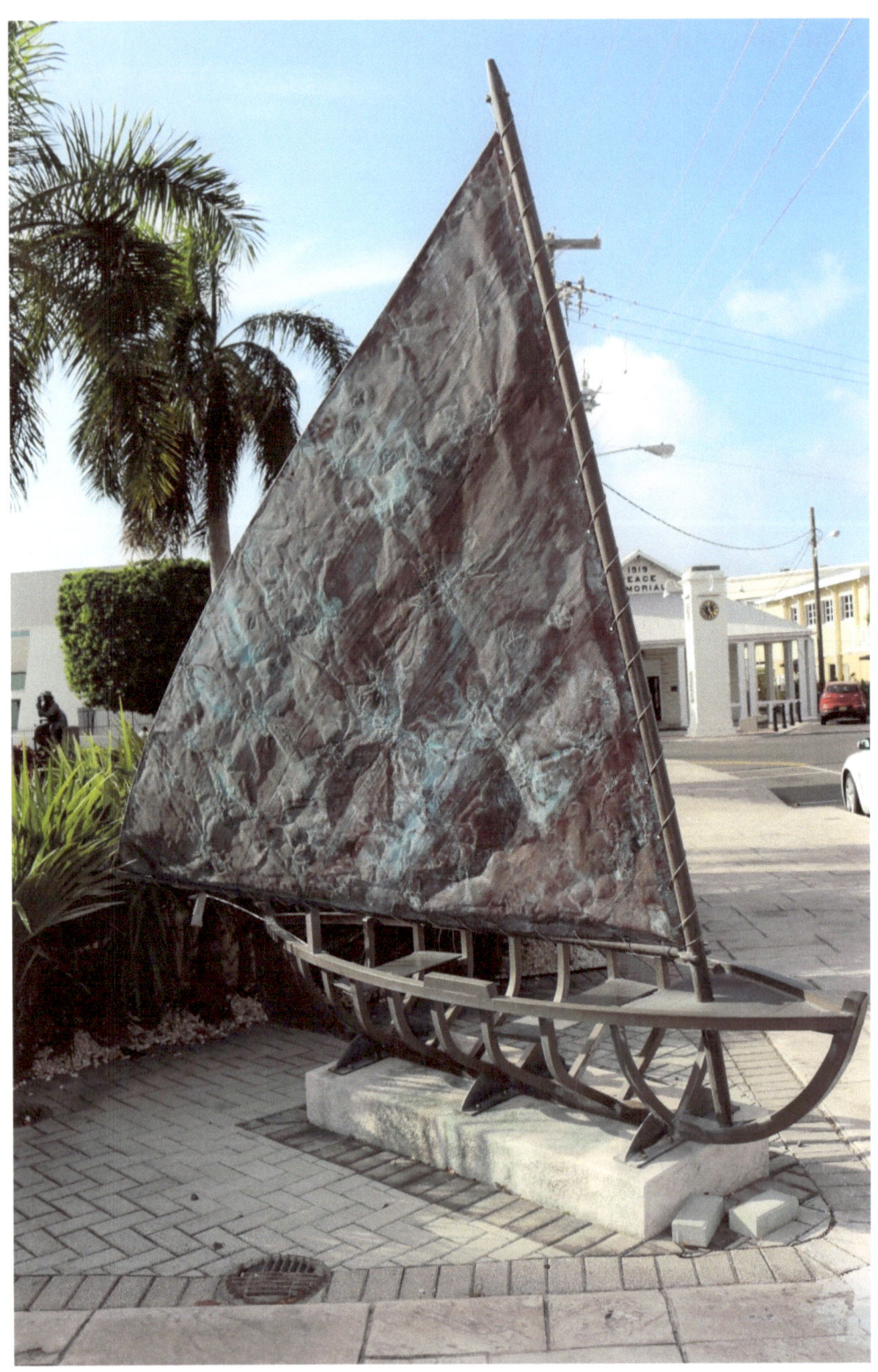

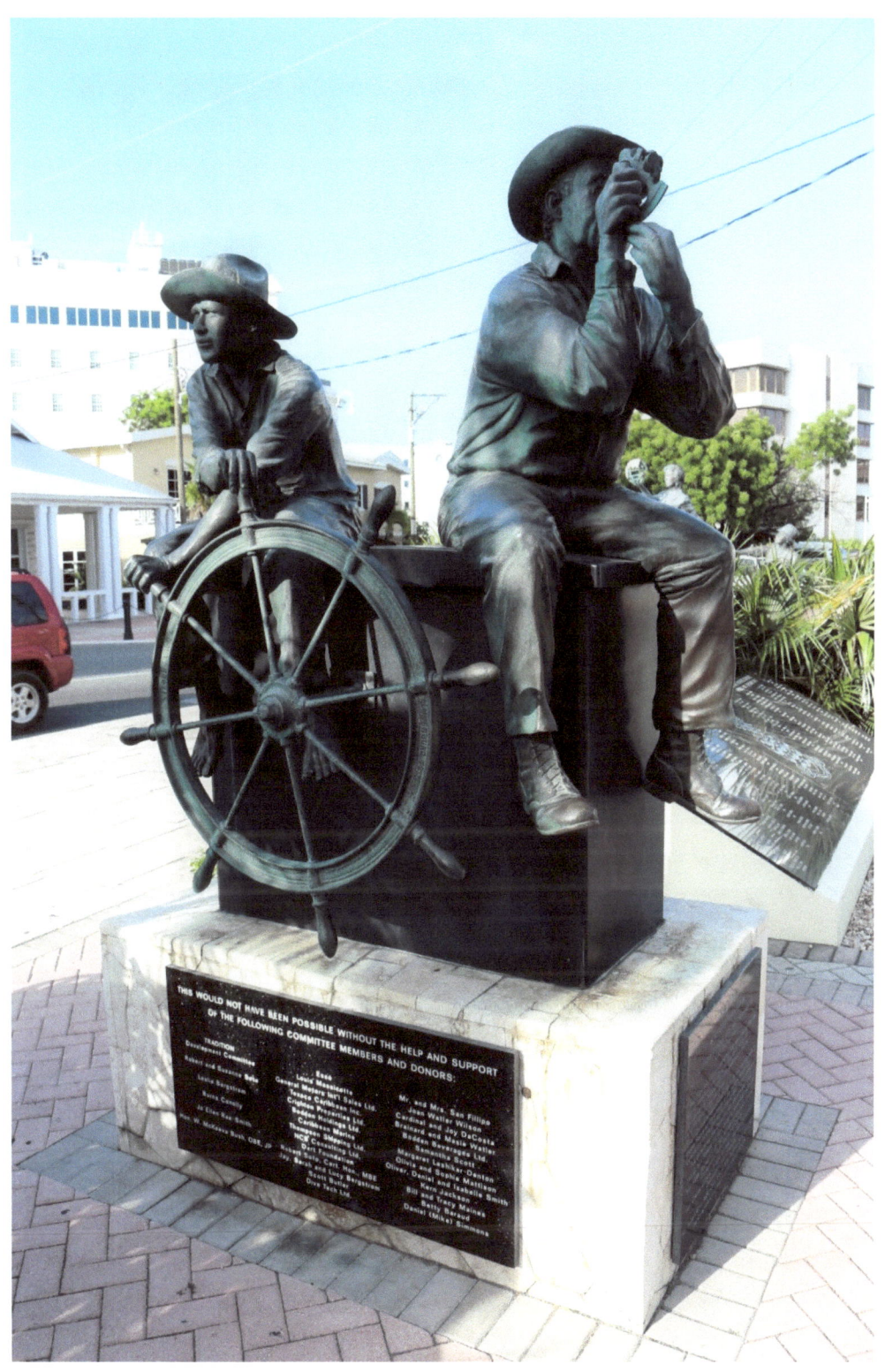

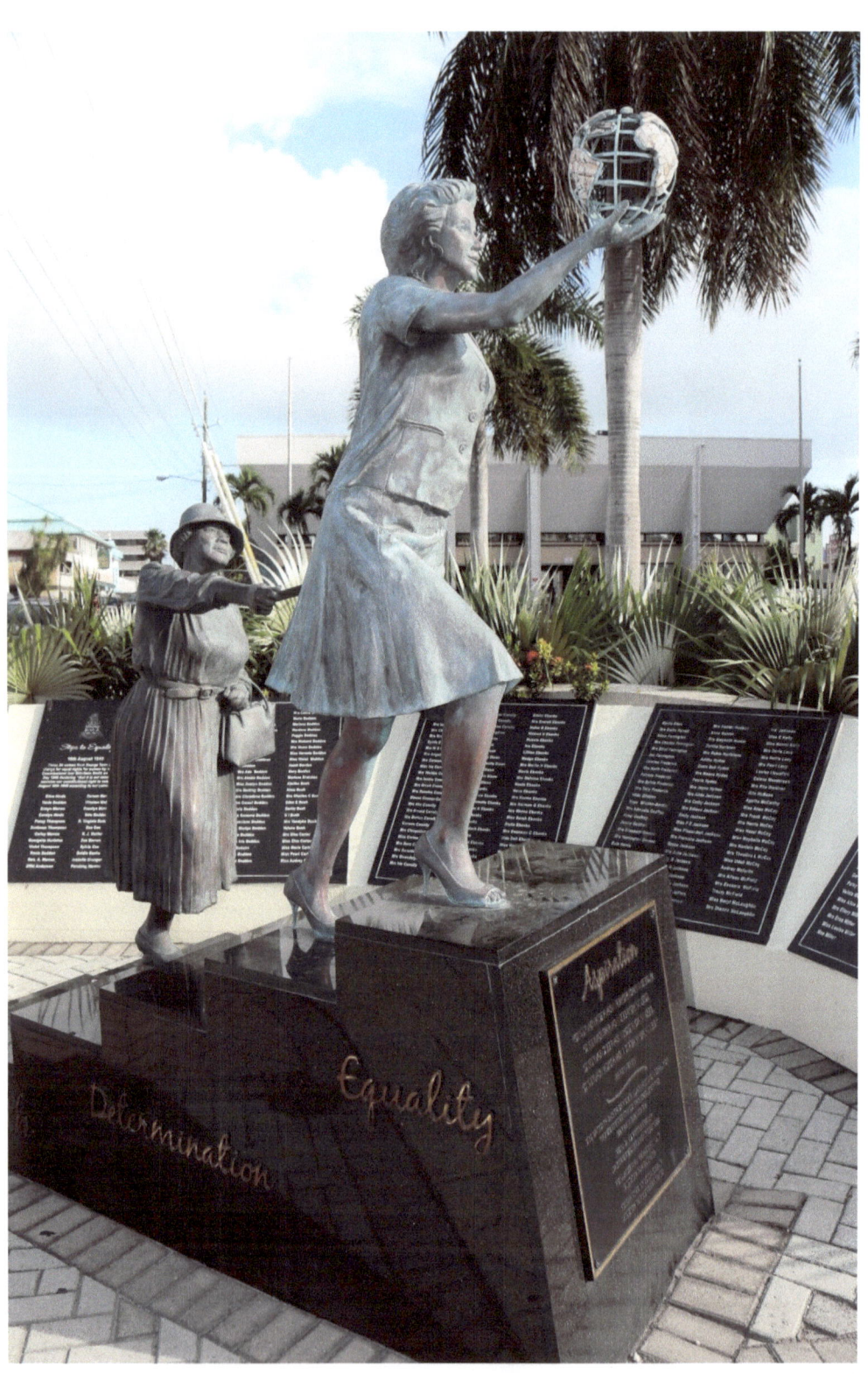

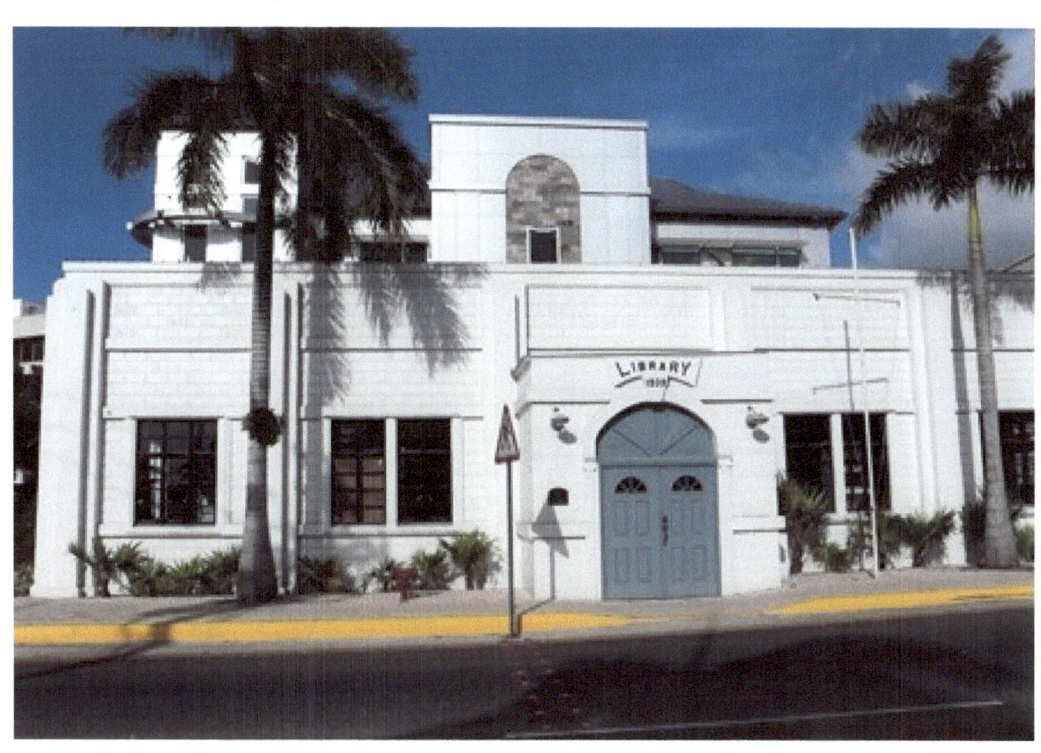

Library and Peace Memorial at the Heroes Square

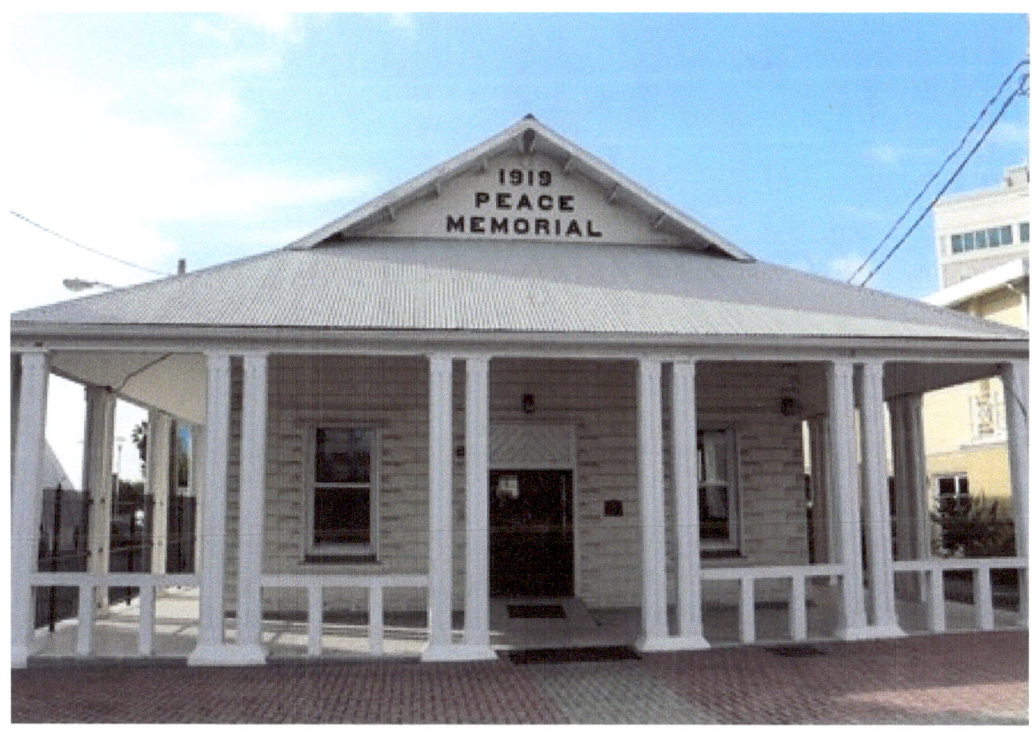

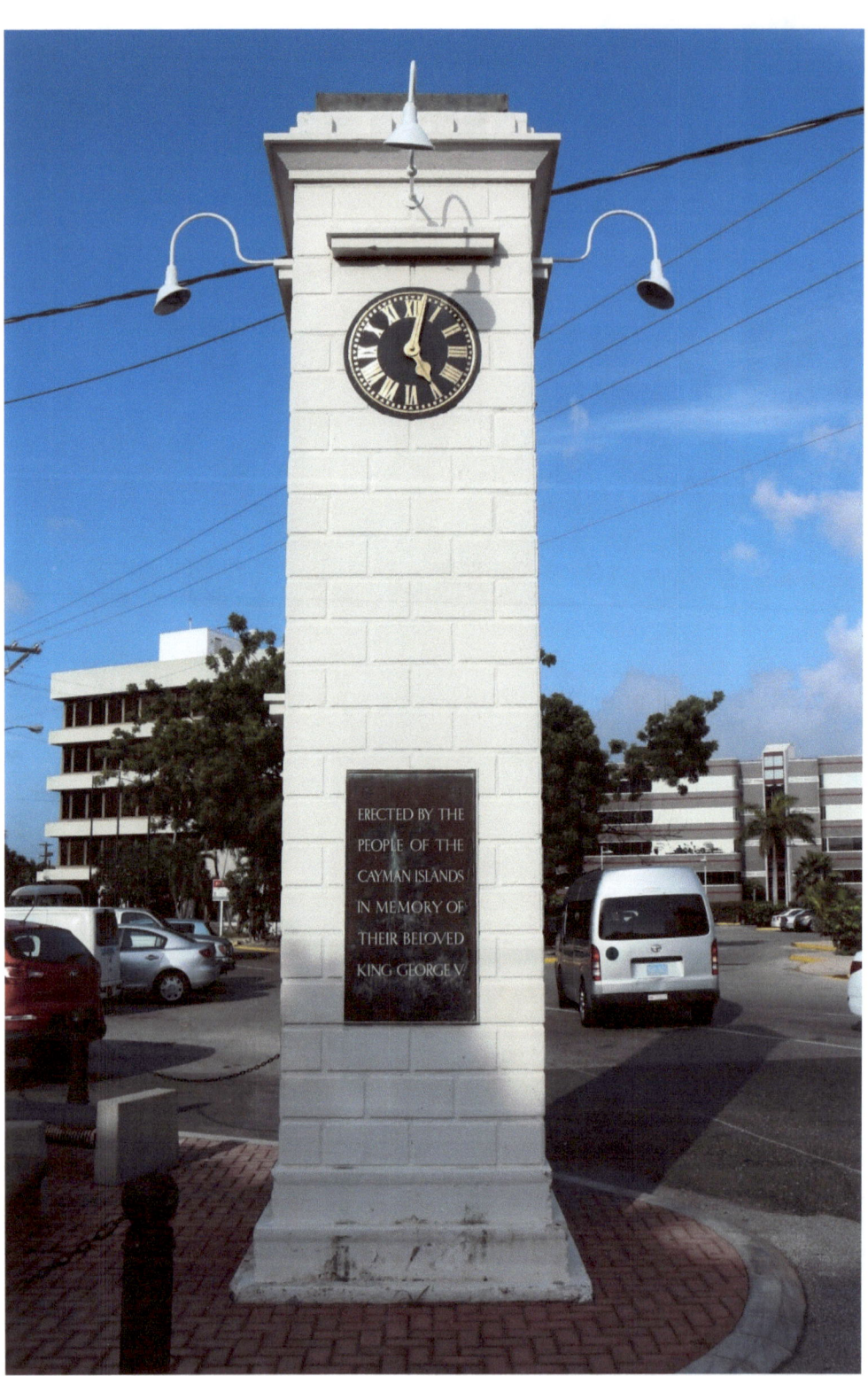

ERECTED BY THE
PEOPLE OF THE
CAYMAN ISLANDS
IN MEMORY OF
THEIR BELOVED
KING GEORGE V

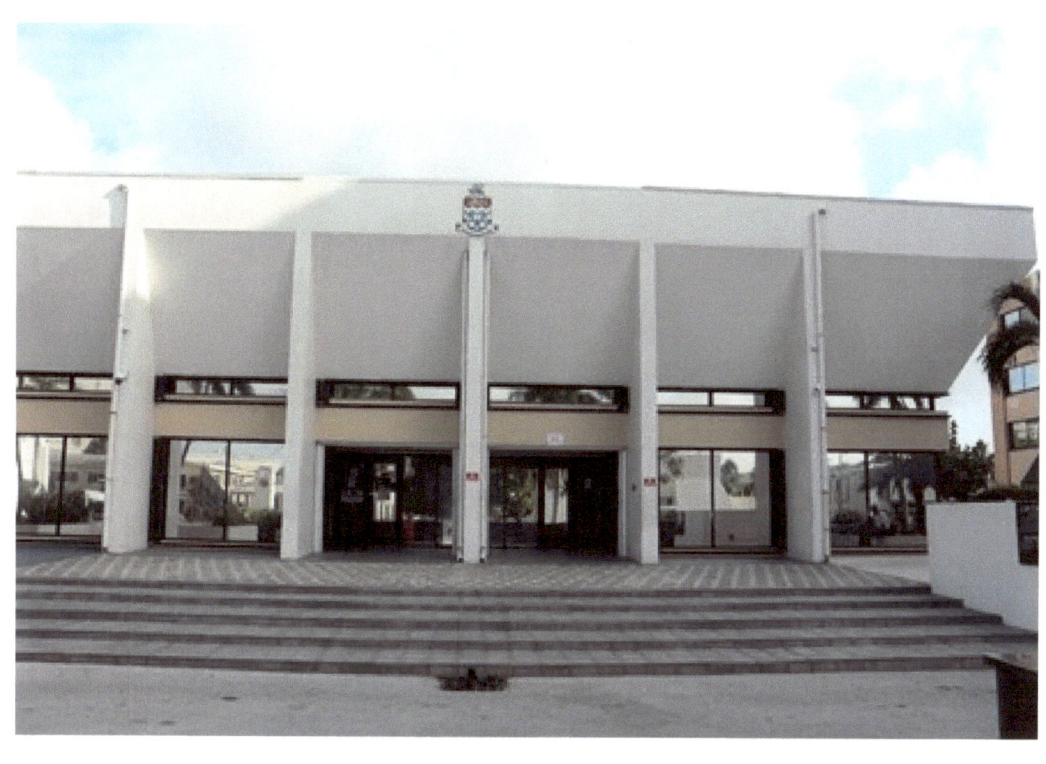

Courthouse and Assembly Hall at the Heroes Square

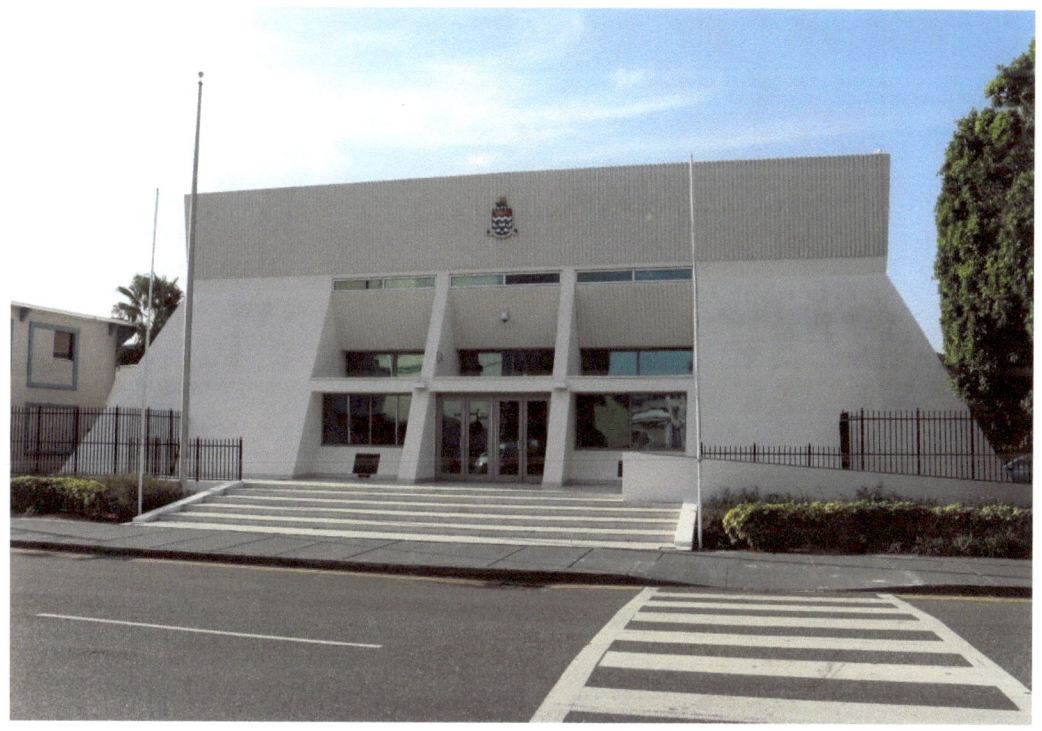

Sunsets in Grand Cayman

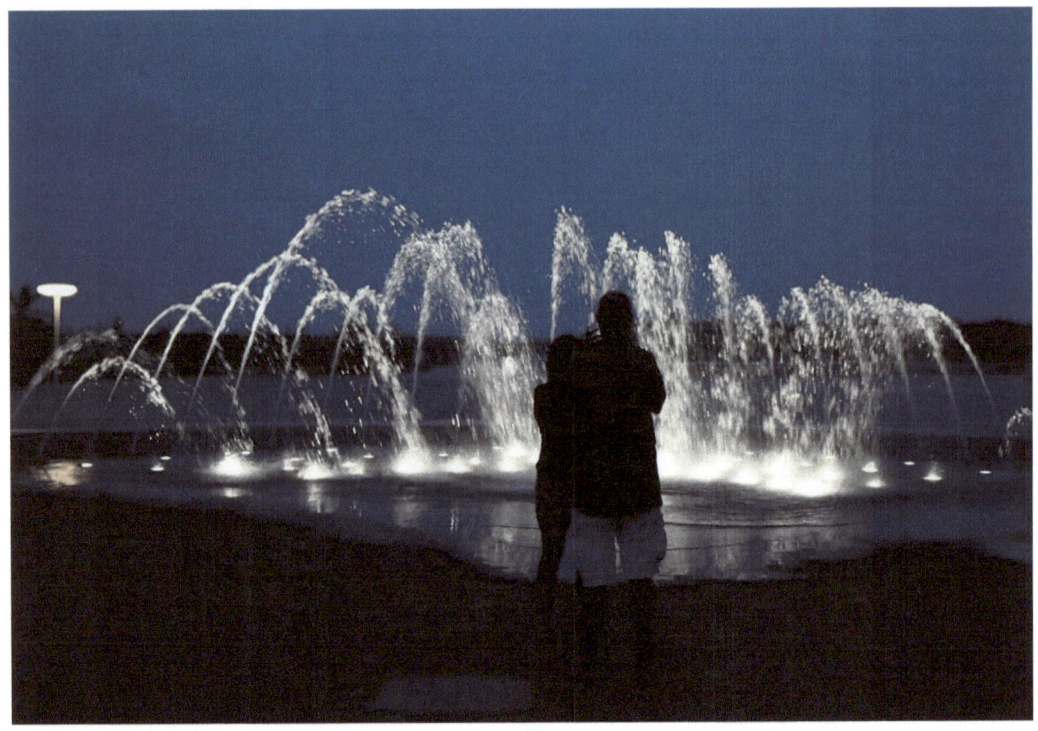

Fountain at Night in Camana Bay

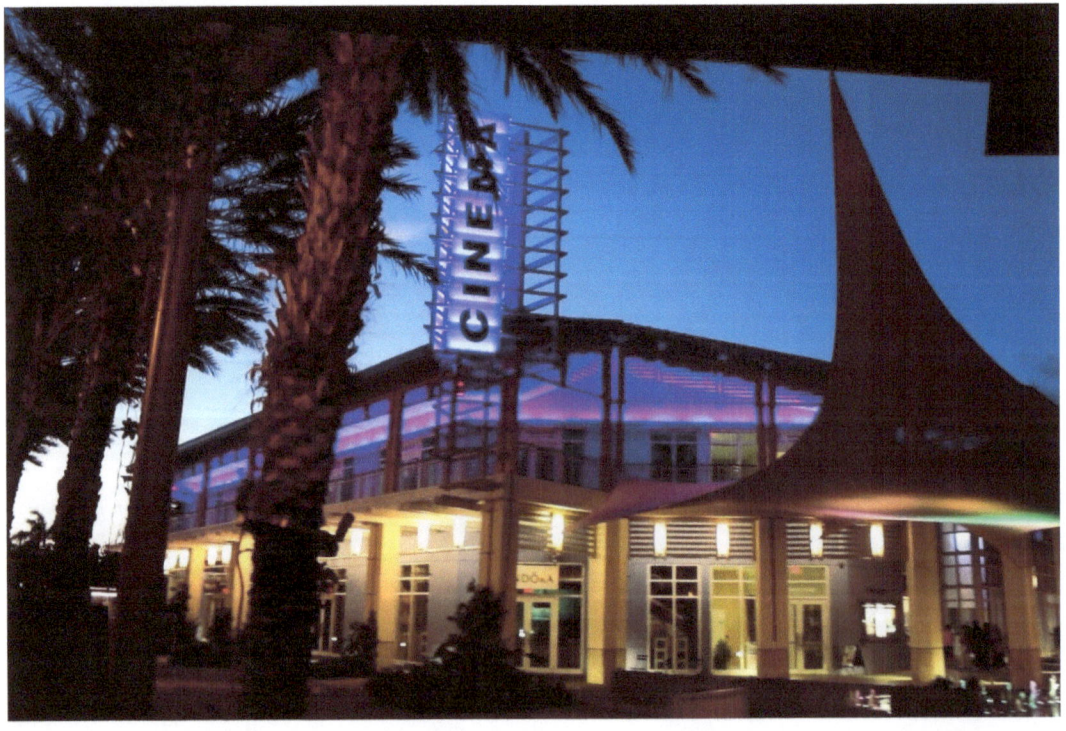

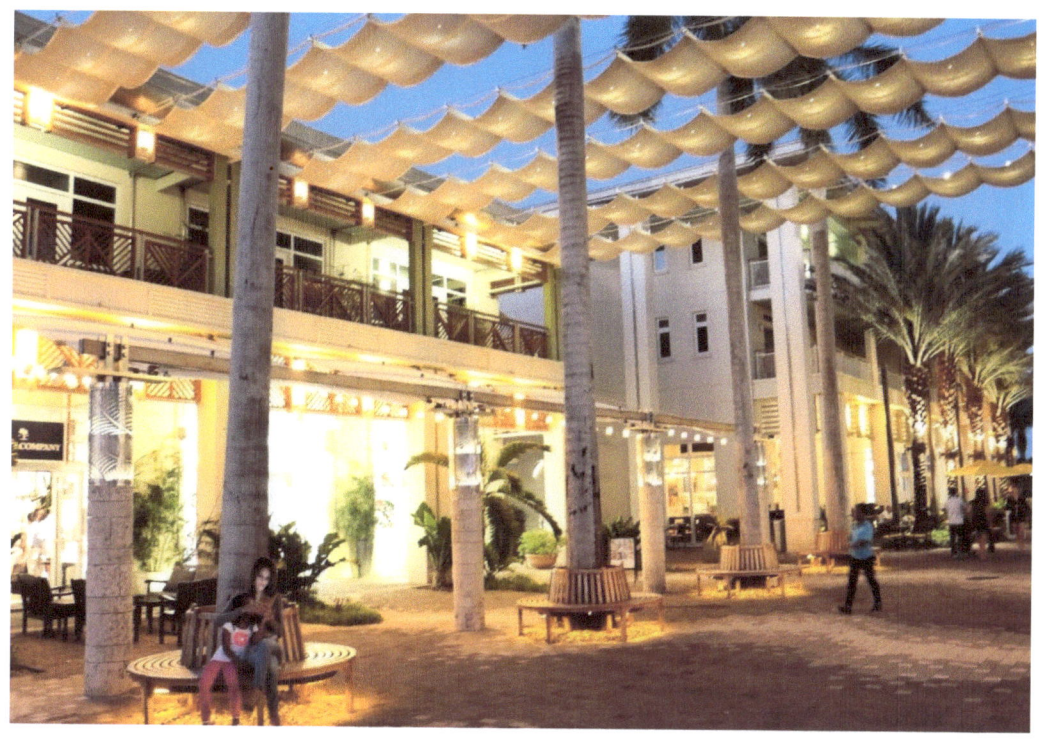

Camana Bay at Night time

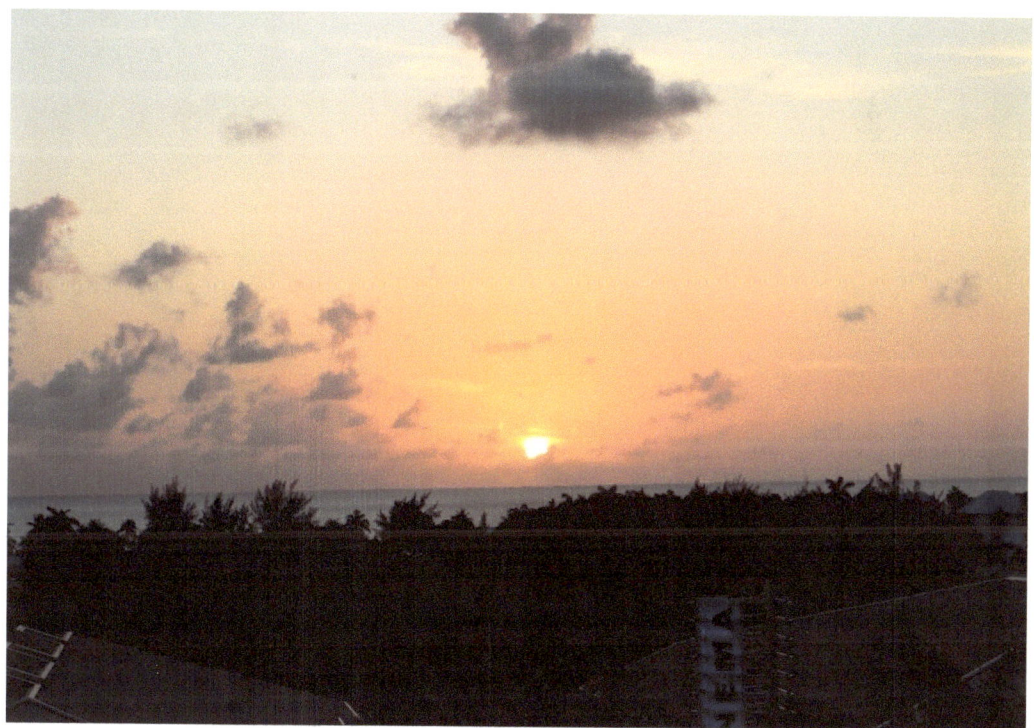

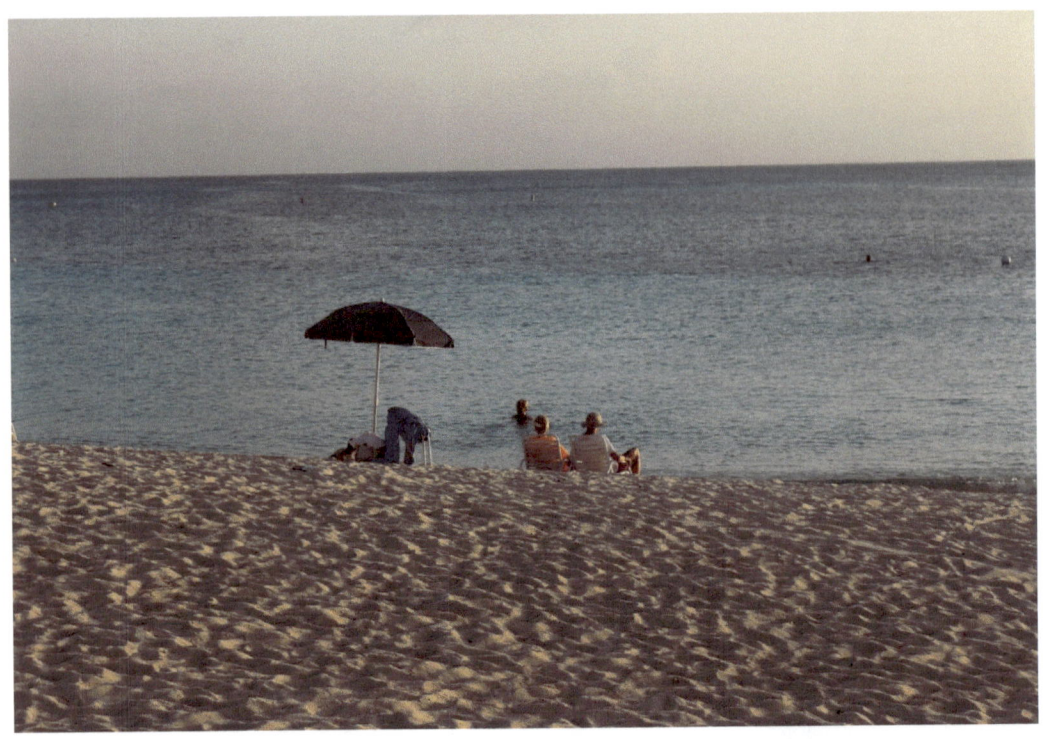

Sunset at the Beach

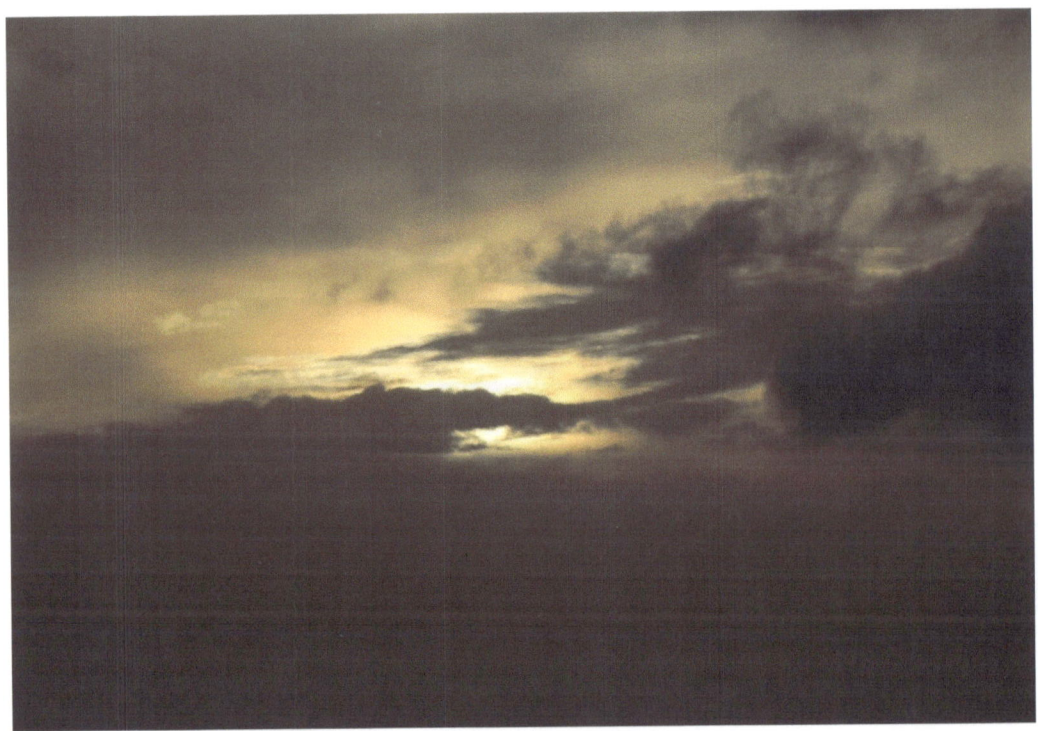

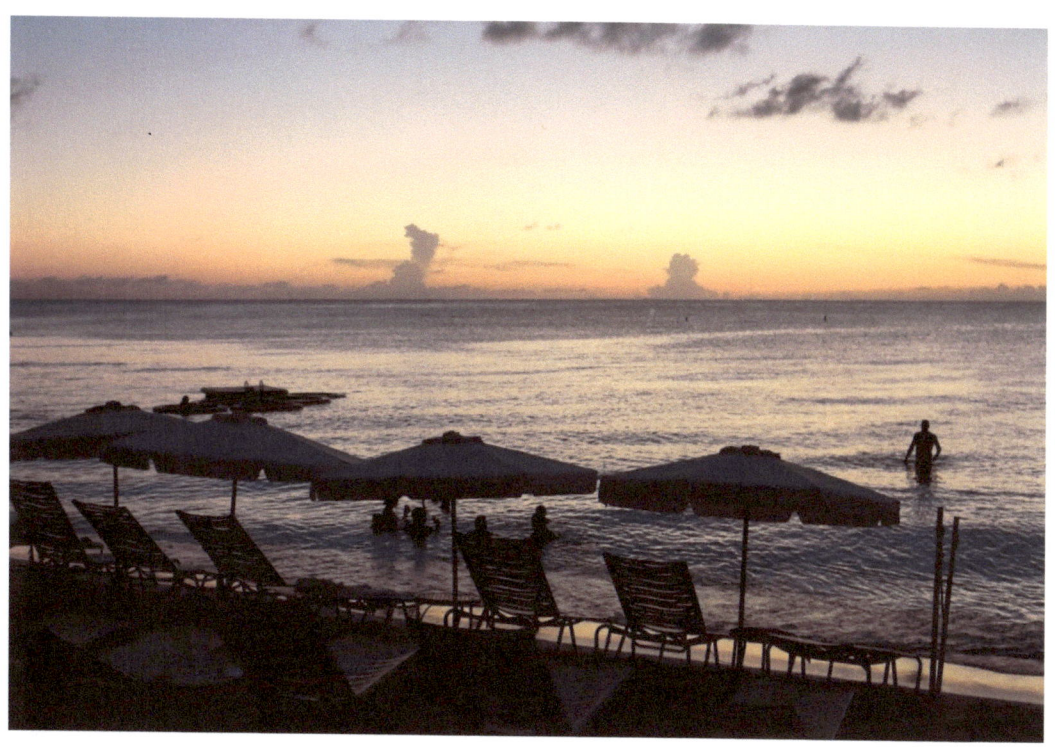

Sunset at the Beach

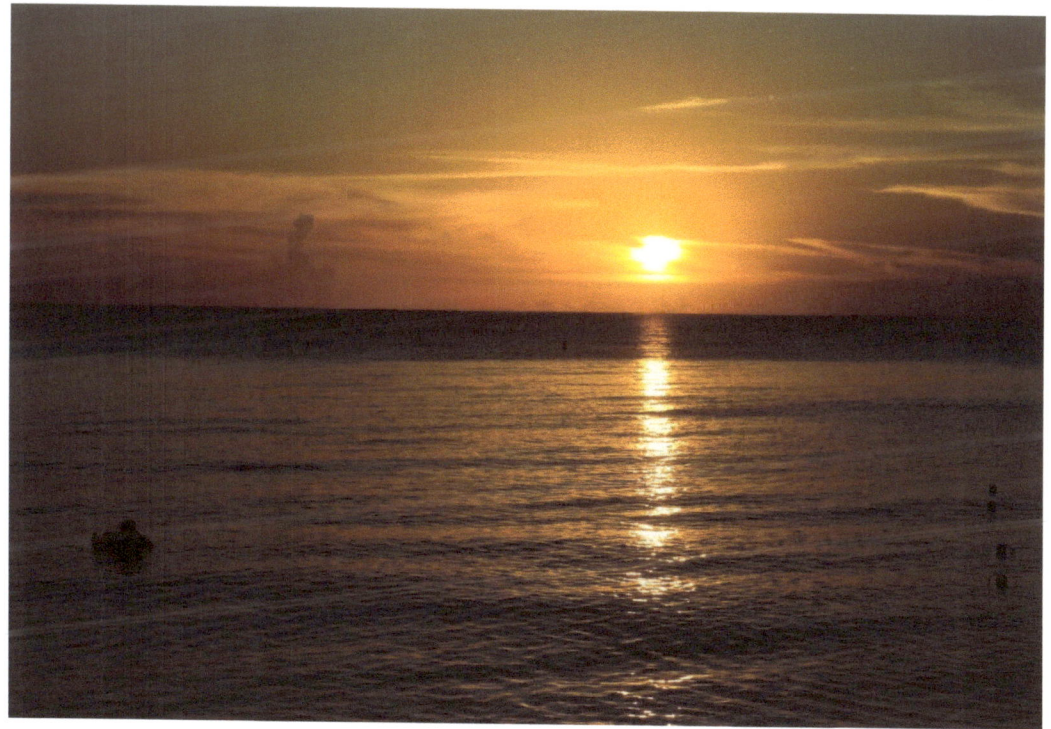

Your Benefits in the Cayman Islands

We hope that we made you curious and you come to Cayman and explore this tropical islands yourself. In this book we show what to expect and to enjoy your life. You now know how to get start and be successful with your business adventure.

These information about your business arrangements and your income related details are protected by the law of the Cayman Islands and you have to take the appropriate taxation steps on your own. However, when your home country investigates your financials in your home country and makes a legal request to the Cayman Islands Department of International Tax Cooperation will cooperate with such an investigation. This is the only authority that will release any of your private information to your home country.

Are you ready to start your adventure in the Cayman Islands?

If the answer is yes, we are happy to assist you! You can reach us at the following websites and email addresses.

- Author website: www.andreahoffdomin.com

- Florida Dream Homes: www.florida-dream-homes.net;
  e-mail: andrea@florida-informations.com

We thank you very much for your interest and your attention in this book. You are always welcome to contact us with questions and notes.

Best wishes from the Caribbean islands and the Sunshine State of Florida!

www.ingramcontent.com/pod-product-compliance
Lightning Source LLC
Chambersburg PA
CBHW050811180526
45159CB00004B/1626